DEFEAT

MEGA-AGENTS

14 SOURCES OF

DIFFERENTIATION

DEFEAT

MEGA-AGENTS

14 SOURCES OF

DIFFERENTIATION

Plus...

A Formula To Be Respected:

**Never Talk To Anyone,
Until They Know
You Are a Someone®**

Ryan Fletcher

DEFEAT MEGA-AGENTS
14 Sources of Differentiation. Plus, A Formula To Be Respected:
Never Talk To Anyone, Until They Know you Are a Someone®

Published by AMS
Printed in the United States of America
ISBN: 1497444764
ISBN-13: 9781497444768

ACKNOWLEDGMENTS

To my little man, Jackson, a.k.a. "Bruce Wayne/Batman," thank you for keeping me on my toes. You are four, but without any real knowledge of how the real world works, or why certain things can't come true or aren't possible, you dare me to think, "Well, what if…" And, without being bound by the universal laws of rational thought and logical reasoning—because you're four, and you still have an imagination that society hasn't stolen from you—you force me to look at the world through a child's eyes. *It's beautiful.*

To my sweetest girl, Zoey, a.k.a. "Wonder Woman", the superhero name assigned to you at birth by your brother. You are a spitfire. One minute you're cuddling and loving your Daddy, the next, you're scratching my face and biting me. At least no one can call you "predictable." And please, never grow up. Never lose your wit. Your sense of humor. Or your natural born personality, to be contrarian to everything, even though you're just 18-months and don't even know what that means. The world doesn't need another lemming. It needs a leader. *Stay awnry!*

To my wife, Melanie, who has given me two beautiful kids and more support than any husband deserves. I thank you. Without support, an entrepreneur is nothing. And, without my kids, I would have no purpose. You have pushed and prodded me. You have inspired me to be a better person. You have been my teammate, in games and battles, you'd rather not have participated in. When I quit jobs. Started new businesses. You've been there for me. Never questioning. Never second-guessing. And, when I've failed, you've never said, "I told you so," even when we both knew it. So, thank you, and please, *keep playing hard to get!* – I like the challenge.

To members of my Protector/Social Superhero program, you too deserve thanks. Without you, this book would not exist. You continue to prove that I'm not crazy. That sophisticated marketing strategies can transform a real estate business, elevate one's status, and even impact the world. Thank you for allowing me to share your stories and breakthroughs. They are inspiring. They are opening the eyes of others, and, most important, they are changing lives. Sometimes all someone needs to see, is what's possible, and you've laid the path.

To my parents, Mom, Dad, thank you for your guidance and support. You've always had my back. And for that, there are no words that can describe my appreciation.

And finally, to the readers of this book, thank you for believing in me, and allowing me to spend the next few hours with you, as we walk side by side, into a world of possibilities.

-Ryan Fletcher

ABOUT THE AUTHOR

It's been said Ryan Fletcher "doesn't look like much" – but clients who've earned millions as direct result of his work, know better than to underestimate him. After 47 straight rejections from medical school, Ryan Fletcher took to real estate. Frustrated by only selling two homes in his first year and having to work part-time as a box boy at UPS to make ends meet, Fletcher pioneered a new approach to client attraction by creating exceptional value for specific clients. This discovery led to an amazing 2100% increase in his year-to-year income. Taking him from $8,846.32 in first year commissions, to $182,972 in his second year—working a fraction of the hours, never on weekends, and with all clients coming to him, required to complete an application just to secure a phone appointment.

Other business owners quickly took notice of Ryan's unique approach and began asking for Fletcher's help. The first marketing campaign he wrote for someone else, paid only $500. It brought such amazing results, though, the client asked him to write another. Fletcher reasoned, if someone was willing to pay him $500 to write a marketing campaign, someone, somewhere, would be willing to pay him $5,000. Never did he imagine someone would be willing to pay him $50,000.00. At just 27 years old, Fletcher received his first $50,000+ check, and three months later, another for $60,000+. He has never looked back.

Today, for obvious reasons, he no longer sells real estate. As of November 2009, when Fletcher semi-retired from private client consulting; new clients were required to go through an initial consulting day at a base rate of $6,800; if, as a result, private client projects were agreed to, compensation typically included fees plus royalties (linked to results) and was not uncommon for project fees to start at $25,000.00 to as much as $50,000.00 for complex, multi-step, multi-media projects. Incredibly, Fletcher has been paid as much as $100,000 in royalties from one sales letter.

His clients have ranged from solo-entrepreneurs to $25,000,000 corporations, to titans in the direct-response industry, like publishing giant Agora Inc., a $500 million/year company. In one 18-month period, Fletcher was directly responsible for more than $25,000,000 in sales for private clients and himself. In head-to-head competitions against the best direct-response copywriters in America, legends like Clayton Makepeace, he's won convincingly, repeatedly. And while many direct-response copywriters dream of writing one million-dollar sales letter in their career, Fletcher, once wrote 5 in a row, selling high priced products / services / positioning service-providers as incredible experts, authority figures, even celebrities among their target markets.

In 2010, with the birth of his son, Jackson Cody Fletcher, and destined to slow down, Mr. Fletcher moved back to quiet Vancouver, WA. This is where he grew up. Within months, Fletcher started his next company, Agent Marketing Syndicate®; where he consulted with, trained and worked closely with entrepreneurial-minded real estate agents—returning to his roots—showing folks in the most commoditized profession on earth, real estate, how to regain control over their time, income and life. Fletcher focused agents on the application (and implementation) of superior marketing and positioning strategies, built into powerful systems, to give them power. He has even trademarked the phrase,

"Never Talk To Anyone, Until They Know You Are a Someone®," because it is the preferred way he and members of his Protector/Social Superhero Program choose to operate their businesses

.

In 2016, Fletcher decided to partner with some of his most passionate students—to launch ImpactClub®; where he is now solely focused. Forging Elite Storytellers™ to compete in the most competitive race on earth. For more information visit: www.StoryAthlete.com. Or for an even more in-depth look: www.90DayImmersion.com

DEFEAT MEGA-AGENTS

TABLE OF CONTENTS

YOU NEED NOT FEAR THE BIG MAN

14 SOURCES OF DIFFERENTIATION TO DEFEAT MEGA-AGENTS

AMPLIFIER STRATEGIES

FOR REAL ESTATE AGENTS WHO WANT TO BE SOMETHING MORE THAN JUST "REAL ESTATE AGENTS"

RESOURCES

BEYOND THE BOOK | 231

DEFEAT MEGA-AGENTS

YOU NEED **NOT**

FEAR

THE

BIG MAN

DEFEAT MEGA-AGENTS

INTRODUCTION
You Need Not Fear The Big Man!

By Ryan Fletcher

In his book *Be Great*, Peter H. Thomas tells the story of two men who are splitting wood. One is 6'6", 250 lbs. and in good physical shape. The other is a scrawny 130 lb. man, with not much muscle. He was, more or less, what's commonly referred to as a "nerd." Anyhow, they started chopping wood at about the same time. When it was time for their morning break, the little guy stopped and took his break. He drank his coffee and relaxed. The big man did not. He kept on working, swinging his axe and splitting wood. The same thing happened when lunchtime rolled around. The little guy stopped and took his break. Ate his sandwich and relaxed, while the big man worked right through lunch. When the afternoon break rolled around, the same thing happened again. This continued for two weeks.

At the end of two weeks, the big 6'6" man was baffled. He had noticed, despite working the extra hours and not taking breaks, he wasn't that far ahead of the nerdy little guy, when it came to the amount of wood each man had split. What made it even more shocking was the fact; the scrawny guy had been leaving at 6 p.m. each day, while the big man often worked til ten or eleven o'clock each night.

After three weeks of this, the big man was demoralized. He had noticed the little man's pile was, more or less, even with his own pile of wood. At the end of the fourth week, the big man was overtaken. Finally, it was just too much for him to take. As the little guy got up from his morning break, the big man said to him, "I cannot understand how you've split more wood than me. You are smaller than I am. You don't have the strength that I have, and your axe is smaller than mine."

The little guy replied, "Yes, my friend, but you never stop to sharpen your axe."

Truth told most business owners and entrepreneurs never sharpen their axe. They wake up each morning, head to the office, and just start swinging. When their axe dulls, or fails to split wood altogether because it was never sharp in the first place, their first thought is to *just* swing harder and harder. All brawn. No brains.

In a survey I conducted over 6 months, when I asked real estate agents: "If you're not currently hitting the income target you've set for yourself, what's the biggest frustration or roadblock preventing you from doing so?" Number one reason, 65.7% said: "Limited budget and resources keep me from competing with Mega-agents i.e. the "big man" in my marketplace." This is sad and pathetic, but also, it is instructive. Mainly because of the fact, had the little guy attempted to compete with the big man, head to head, stroke for stroke, muscle vs. muscle, doing exactly as the big man did, he would have lost. But he didn't.

By stopping and taking his breaks, to refuel and to sharpen his axe, he baffled the big man and defeated him working only a fraction of the time. This book, Defeat Mega-Agents, is all about sharpening your axe. Most of us are the "little guy" in the marketplace and must find ways, David vs. Goliath, to defeat the big man. On a consulting call with a private client, I asked one simple but very important eight-word question:

What benefit do you bring to your marketplace?

For a second he was silent. Then he started talking to himself. It was clear, answering this question was difficult for him. He said he really had to stop and think about it. He said, "I know I provide great service. I know have a great product, and that I have a great deal of knowledge that can help people," but then, again, he went quiet. After several minutes, he said, "But none of that makes me unique because that's what everyone [all my competitors] say too." Then he continued, "So really, how the hell am I any different?"

I said to him "That's the riddle we must solve."

I urge you to ask yourself that same question: "What (unique) benefit do you bring to the marketplace, that differentiates you from the "big man" you must compete against, and all the other competitors in your industry, and area, that compete against you?"

Seriously, take 20 minutes to think about that. Stop reading. Ask yourself:

- What different and unique benefit do I bring to the table?

- As a business owner and entrepreneur, as a real estate agent—what do I do for my client(s) that is so different, so profound and effective that justifies my existence in the marketplace?

- Why do I even deserve to be in the marketplace, with all those other players, to suck up air and take up space?

Without a good answer to those questions, you will forever be stuck going head-to-head with the big man, stroke for stroke, in a battle you likely can't win.

In my past life when I was a real estate agent, I went to great lengths to construct powerful answers to those questions. For those who don't know, real estate is a Negative Reputation industry, which means, basically, people hate you before they know you, and distrust you before you speak a word. This is true of virtually all "sales"-related industries because of the public's distaste for salespeople. This is, by the way, why most people fail in these industries too. They never figure out how to overcome this odds-against-them starting point, where the black chips of *anti*-trust are stacked against them. But using the precise strategies revealed in this book, I did. And in doing so, I was been able to operate my business, as my members and clients are able to operate their businesses today, in a way that most my competitors deemed impossible.

Here is the TRUTH about Defeating Mega-agents:

When you sell a commodity, which is what most products are, which are what most professional services are, where the perception is that you, and every service-provider in that industry, i.e. real estate, do the exact same thing and/or sell the exact same product—your challenge is to find a way to change the rules of the game so you appear different from competitors—even if you sell, fundamentally, the same product or offer the exact same service. In other words, if you can't alter the product or service to gain a competitive advantage, you must alter something else.

In this book, you and I (we) are going to confront and analyze fourteen complex and sophisticated ways to "alter something else" as a pathway to true differentiation in your business.

Now, fair warning.

These strategies are not magic, fairytale simple. Most business owners and entrepreneurs, especially, most real estate agents, would prefer that I provide a new, simple 8 or 9 word phrase or slogan that can be "turned on" like a vibrator, to immediately start bringing them increased client counts and profit. I don't blame you. I too wish this "simple cure" were available for me, in my different businesses. But I'm not Alice, this isn't Wonderland, and I don't possess any magical rabbit capable of fulfilling that wish.

The Business Lesson My Dad Taught Me:

When I turned sixteen, my Dad unknowingly taught me one of the greatest business lessons of my life. For my first car, he did me a favor and "privileged me" with a shiny "new" 1980 Volkswagen rabbit. It cost $500. The paint was red, but badly faded and chipped.

When I crawled inside, it was clear why it was only $500 bucks. The dash was cracked. Both seats had tears in them. The floorboards had holes in the carpet. Mildew filled the air. It was a strong scent. The passenger wing window had been busted out, fixed, with Plexiglas and duct tape. Two of the three control knobs were missing on the radio, and the more you looked at, and examined, the more you noticed was broken. The best part about the whole car was that it only leaked a little oil, not a lot. There was only a small hole in the muffler, not a big one.

To be fair, could I have improved the car, at least its appearance, with a new paint job? *Sure.* And this is what my Dad said to me, "Take it down to Macco." But as I told my Dad, even with a new paint job, "it would still be a 1980 Volkswagen rabbit that looks like hell and smells like shit inside." And, trust me, this did not go unnoticed to the girls I dated. Or tried to date.

The point is, of course, and the lesson my Dad made clear to me: You can't hope to fix a broken leg with a Band-Aid.

If you're not hitting the income targets you've set for yourself, if clients are not flowing to you as freely and as easily as you'd like them to, or if you find yourself spending too much in marketing and advertising or have to chase prospects to acquire new clients for your business, then radical changes might be necessary.

When I said we'd be sharpening our axe, what I really meant was we'll be throwing the damn axe away and building a mill. Big saws. Lots of electricity. Profound difference.

It's my contention with the ever-worsening commoditization of almost every industry and category of business, from consumer products and professional services, and everything from entertainment to manufacturing, given the vast array of new, and ever-expanding options that are available to the consumer and client—not just a fresh coat a paint—but a new car—is what's necessary and required moving forward, to prosper. Especially in real estate, and, especially if your goal and ambition is to defeat Mega-agents that have sizable marketing budgets that you do not.

This book is, therefore, an opportunity manual.

Don't just read it. Use it. Work with it. If you are a serious entrepreneur, not just "playing one" in real estate, then you know what that word means: *work*. But trying to match the big guy, stroke for stroke, with no strategic advantage—all brawn, no brain—is just plain *fucking* stupid.

Don't worry, I can say that. I grew up in a construction family. My Dad was a homebuilder and my uncles own a concrete company. On the job site, every other word is a four letter word, and after awhile, each four letter word is just another word.

One thing about me, I believe in being authentic. And from time to time, that's how I talk. *Bluntly.* And to the point.

So let's get to it.

Editorial Notes:

- Throughout the book, periodically, I'll be referring to members of my Protector/Social Superhero program, as P/SS members. (In 2018, that program was significantly altered to serve and impact a greater audience on a larger scale).

- No attempt has been made at politically correct gracefulness, or perfect grammar, or evening out "he" and "she" or constantly saying "she and he" and "he and she." I'm not getting paid by the word. You'll find "he" used throughout as convenience, not as slight.

Recommended Resources:

• **Protector Videos Series** (Access inside Member Site)

• **Case Study Interviews** (Access inside Member Site)

• **AMS Podcast** (www.AMSpodcast.com)

• **Value-Driven Approach** (www.TheValueDrivenApproach.com)

• **Forging Elite Storytellers** (www.StoryAthlete.com)

• **90-Day Immersion** (www.90DayImmersion.com)

• **Explore ImpactClub®** (www.ImpactClub.com)

DIFFERENTIATION

TO DEFEAT

MEGA-AGENTS

Plus...
A Formula To Be Respected:

NEVER TALK TO ANYONE, UNTIL THEY KNOW YOU ARE A SOMEONE®

ONE

SOURCE OF
DIFFERENTIATION #1
Niche Marketing

By Ryan Fletcher

T rying to be all things to all people is a losing proposition. Yet, 99% of business owners ignore this most basic truth. I am here to tell you, any real estate agent or entrepreneur resistant to changing their modus operandi from the traditional "any warm body with a pulse" mentality, to laser-beam focus on a certain niche, like the Dodo bird, will soon be an extinct.

Does Interstate Department Store mean anything to you? Yes? No? Doesn't really matter, all you need to know is that it went bankrupt. After years of hemorrhaging money, the company looked at its books and decided to focus on the only product it made money on: Toys. They then did something smart. Since Interstate made the decision to focus *solely* on toys, it changed its name to 'Toys "R" Us' to reflect its new niche. How about that name, certainly you recognize it? Toys "R" Us now does 20% of the retail toy business in the country. If you look at which retailers are in trouble today, it's the department stores: The *Generalists*. Macys, the world's largest department store, several years ago, filed for bankruptcy.

JC Penny and Sears are now on life support, working quickly to re-tool for survival. These generalists apparently did not learn the lesson of Interstate Department Store.

Folks, this is a powerful trend. In every category of business, product and service, the shift from generalist to specialist is evident.

On television there is no longer just one general cooking show. The Food Network has more than a dozen different specialized shows; one for every interest: Cakes, wedding cakes, cupcakes, cake competitions, etc. ESPN is one of the constant innovators in broadcasting. They have not ignored this trend either. In recent years they've moved from just a *general* ESPN.com to catering to specific fans and niches, ESPNBoston.com, ESPNDallas.com, ESPNLosAngeles.com, ESPNChicago.com, and others.

Unless you're an automobile buff, you've probably never heard of the monthly magazine called *Hemmings Motor News*. But while *general* newspapers like the *New York Times* and *Washington Post*, both of which sold recently for less than 10% of their value from just a decade ago—are dying on the vine—Hemmings sells 265,000 copies a month and grosses $20 million a year. The owner of *Hemmings Motor News*, Terry Ehrich, says his publication is "one of publishing's great cash cows." He says, "I'm just a mediocre jockey on a helluva horse." A horse that just happens to be a helluva niche publication, serving a niche population of *old-school* car buffs who love them some muscle cars.

Face it, we now live in a "There's an app for that" world.

Fifty years ago general information was fine. Choices were limited.

For the nightly news, you could tune into one of just three channels. *General* programs were fine. Back then, Colgate only made one toothbrush too, and it worked just fine for everyone. But now, fast forward 50 years, if you're a heterosexual, Caucasian, age 45 to 50, have one short leg, one bad eye, you have crooked teeth, gingivitis and off-white but not quite yellow teeth, with sensitive gums and foul smelling breathe – guess what? Yep. One of those 200 specialized toothbrushes that Colgate now makes, requiring two full store aisles just to shelve, is "Just for you." Made for you. Customized for you. Exclusively caters to you, and your oral problems.

Remember when a toothbrush was just a toothbrush? Those were the good ole days, but nobody wants a general toothbrush anymore, or anything else general. Times have changed. The Internet and the mass proliferation of technology and different publishing platforms like Facebook, and iTunes, allow people to only pay attention to the things that they are keenly interested in. People only want what they judge to be "just right" *and* perfect "for them."
They want to be able to look at a product or service and instantly know, "This is for me." This desire for customization, applies to every aspect of their life.

I created my Niche Only Program® concept—specialized real estate services for different niches; teachers, military, nurses, fireman, and police officers—to capitalize on this trend. *WHO* you are selling to—the niche you choose—is *more* important than anything else. If you have a "farm" of chickens, cows, pigs, ducks, mice, rodents and 37 other kinds of critters, it is damn hard to feed everyone the *right* food, perfectly suited "for them." But if you've got only cattle, or only pigs, or only chickens, and, if you've ever seen the controversial documentary *'Food Inc.'*, then you know just how easy it is, and can be, to craft the perfect *hormone-cocktail* perfectly suited for just that animal, to maximize its growth.

This same truth can be applied to all businesses and sales professions. You need a "farm" of one kind of animal. Only then can you craft the perfect diet, the perfect *Marketing Message*, to maximize growth, response from that *target* niche.

The vast majority of ordinary business owners with ordinary incomes and a never-ending list of ordinary complaints about how hard they work, with so little to show for it, have this in common: They have a farm of 37 different kinds of animals. And they're trying to feed all 37 animals the same food. Here's the problem: Deer don't like cheese. Rats do. And rats don't like salt licks, deer do. Solution: Get rid of 34 or 35 or 36 of the 37 animals, and get really good at cooking just one, two, or three "special dishes" perfectly suited for those two to three carefully selected niches.

I am here to tell you, the biggest leverage you're going to find: Taking small amounts of money and getting big results. Small amounts of effort and getting big results – is learning, understanding and implementing niche marketing.

It is very simple: "Riches in Niches" is how you Defeat Mega-agents.

Niche marketing is where the money is. Nobody else in your marketplace practices niche marketing. Not correctly. By doing so, you clearly identify your products and services, your business, and yourself as the specialist "for them." The response you want from people when they see your marketing and advertising is for them to say, if not aloud, at least in their head, "This is for me."

Should you need to prove to yourself how powerful this trend has become, just stroll down the vitamin aisle on your next visit to the grocery store.

Better yet, pay a visit to GNC: Vitamins for women. Vitamins for men. Vitamins for athletes. Vitamins for male athletes. Vitamins for female athletes. Vitamins 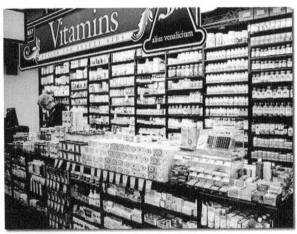 for seniors. Vitamins for active seniors. Vitamins for active seniors with osteoporosis. Vitamins for pilots to promote vision and eye health. Vitamins for weight management. Vitamins for strong hair, skin and nails. Vitamins for sexual well-being. Vitamins for joint and muscle support. Vitamins for brain and memory support. Vitamins for detox and cleanse. Vitamins for stress management. Vitamins for blood sugar support. Vitamins for sleep support. Vitamins for cardiovascular support. Vitamins for focus and clarity. Etc. And folks, these are just categories. Within each category there is another dozen or more specific options, each catering to and promising specialized benefits.

The more narrowly defined the niche is, the more *specific* we can customize the "bait" to catch only that specific kind of fish we wish to catch. Not to mention, the more powerful *that* bait becomes because, as Dan Kennedy calls it, its **message-to-market** match.

Exclusive Niche Marketing, is the *foundation* on which all other forms of differentiation can be built. In the pages that follow (Figure 1-1 through 1-5) are several of the first ads I ever wrote, catering to niches, after discovering this concept. After a year of failure and only selling two homes in my first 12 months, in my first sixty days of niche marketing, I put almost $40,000 in commissions under contract. Chris Spivey (See Figure 1-6) is one whose business has been changed by the creation of a Niche Only Program® as well. Experiencing back-to-back record years, he's donated thousands of dollars to First Responder-connected charities and foundations. Chris also use to be a First Responder, prior to getting into real estate, so he thoroughly speaks their language.

"Riches in Niches"

It's not a myth. It's the truth.

Relevant Podcast Episodes: 5, 23, 73, 86

<u>Recommended Resources:</u>

• **Protector Videos Series** (Access inside Member Site)

• **Case Study Interviews** (Access inside Member Site)

• **AMS Podcast** (www.AMSpodcast.com)

• **Forging Elite Storytellers** (www.StoryAthlete.com)

FIGURE 1-1: Niche Teacher Ad

"New Program Helps Vancouver Teachers Discover Hidden Profits Buried In Their Home!"

By Amber Reneau / staff writer

"Vancouver teacher's now have a better option to increase profits from the sale of their home," that's what third grade teacher Melanie Egger said after participating in Ryan Fletcher's New Teacher Only Program™.

It's not all that often when you hear a feel good story in this day and age – with the media constantly touting the possibility of a recession, rising gas prices, or the battered state of the real estate market – which is why I've chosen to spotlight Ryan Fletcher who is making a difference in teacher's lives and bank accounts.

"The Teacher Only Program™ is not for lawyers, doctors, plumbers, engineers, carpet cleaners or any other profession!"

Always underpaid, and even less appreciated, our teachers are amongst the most affected by the current "credit/gas/recession" crisis. And despite having a college degree (or better) many of our young and even veteran teachers are facing tough times ahead.

With foreclosures and housing inventory at an all time high, compounded by a sharp decline in consumer spending, many teachers who need (or want) to sell their home, risk losing thousands of dollars – but there is a solution, and many teachers have already discovered it.

Ryan Fletcher, of Keller Williams Realty, runs what he calls "a teacher friendly program". Fletcher specializes in helping Vancouver-area teachers as his way of giving back to the educators who have not been properly rewarded for their hard work – and to a profession that (arguably) impacts more lives than any other!

He explains, "I was inspired to create the Teacher Only Program™ after having met up with a friend of mine and nine other teachers for weekend happy hour."

"When you get nine teachers around one table, wine glasses full, and there's no hush-hush – the conversation gets pretty interesting."

Ryan says colorfully, "Girls gone wild!" He continues, "Maybe I was naïve, I don't know, but I never realized all the politics and "b.s." teachers have to put up with / how teachers are 'controlled' by what they can or can't do depending on where the funding (or grant money) comes from for a particular program.

Fletcher has a point. In recent years, teachers have been restricted in their style of teaching to become almost robot-like, working from pre-scripted guidelines aimed (only) at improving standardized test scores. And it's a shame, because teachers are being robbed of their talent and from using their training, hard-work and creativity to invent their own style.

"Our teachers are being taken advantage of – and that's just wrong!"

Fletcher says, "it's no secret teachers aren't rewarded properly for their hard-work – so when they're continually being hit up to attend even more meeting, get more education and work more hours, for a salary that warrants them to only a couple hundred dollar raise each year – that's just wrong," exclaims Fletcher!

"Not to mention, how much (of their own money) teachers spend on materials, supplies, holiday parties, and other miscellaneous stuff for their classrooms just so "our kids" can benefit. Maybe this doesn't surprise you, but I was shocked by how commonplace all this really is."

The sad part, Ryan says, "Is the fact almost every one of the teachers he spoke to, expressed that the hassles of being a teacher has diluted their love for working with children. Some even expressed the want to quit teaching, but said they had no other choice. Stating, they had already committed 4 years of their life getting a degree in education, so what other option did they have?"

He continues, "And what's worse is the fact that the school system knows this, and uses their dedication to their job, and commitment "our kids" to justify the little "weasel" moves that take place each day.

How teachers should work more and get paid less "for the kids." How by paying teachers less they can hire more educators, invest in better schools, upgrade equipment, etc. "for the kids!"

"Seems to me, they should pay you what you're really worth and allocate a bigger portion of the budget to all that other stuff"

Ryan says proudly, "Teachers shouldn't be punished, they should be rewarded – and that's why I created the Teacher Only Program™ and why it's offered exclusively to teachers!"

"Maybe the teachers I hung out with where a bunch of cynics, I don't know, but I doubt it, says Fletcher. This type of stuff happens everywhere, and to other teachers like you, who don't deserve it!"

Ryan is the real deal. Before agreeing to do this article I did my homework. After all – the real estate community hasn't exactly earned the most trustworthy reputation.

Too good to be true?

Nope. Ryan checked out and passed with flying colors. And his past clients seem to love him. In fact, one elderly lady told me, if she didn't already have 17 grandchildren she'd adopt Ryan as her own!

Fletcher says, "I don't blame people for being skeptical, that's human nature. But the Teacher Only Program™ has been so successful because it fixed everything that was missing."

Ryan has been criticized by other agents, brokers, and even the association for his "outside-the-box" style of effective advertising, but claims, "I don't care. I created this program to provide our hard-working (and all too often under-appreciated) teachers with a competitive edge in today's struggling real estate market. So I don't mind if I have to step on a few (political) toes to make that happen!"

Fletcher is a real "hands on guy" dedicated to helping our teachers generate more profit from the sale of their home – plain and simple!

If you, or a teacher you know is interested in learning more about the Teacher Only Program™ Ryan has been kind enough to create a Free 28-Page Report titled, *How Teachers Can Simply & Easily Discover The Hidden Profits Buried In Their Home Sale!*

Ryan explains, by putting every detail into a FREE Report, teachers can enjoy a pressure-free environment (in their own home) while the study the specifics, see the proof, determine if they qualify, and ultimately make their own decision whether (or not) the Teacher Only Program™ is right for them."

You can claim your FREE copy by visiting the teacher only website at ▬▬▬▬▬▬ or through Ryan's 24-hour teacher only hotline at 1-800-▬▬▬▬▬ by simply leaving your name and mailing address – and don't worry, no one will ever call.

Fletcher says, "And if you don't think I can help you, just visit ▬▬▬▬▬▬ and look at the testimonials from the other Vancouver teachers I've already helped – and please know, you can get the very same help!"

Fletcher is a life-long Vancouver resident, a financial supporter of the VSD, volunteers at SW Medical Center, and is a member of the Chamber of Commerce. His mom teaches a parenting class at Clark College, and he lives in Hazel Dell with his wife Melanie and puppy "Lola"

FIGURE 1-2: Niche LGBT Ad

"New Program Helps Vancouver's LGBT Community Find Hidden Profits Buried In Their Home Sale!"

By Amber Reneau / staff writer

In an industry dominated by stereotypes and negative public perception – where realtors are often referred to as under-trained and over-paid, crooks, thieves, unethical – one local realtor has been strong advocate against what he calls a flawed system, and now, is helping Vancouver's LGBT community escape the real estate "rat race" once and for all.

His name is Ryan Fletcher. He's a realtor with Keller Williams Realty – and also, the creator of the LGBT Only Program™.

"The LGBT Only Program™ offers gay and lesbian couples the ability to sell their home without being judged!"

"People don't understand what gay and lesbian couples have to deal with on a daily basis – the idea of being "tolerated" by the public as if they shouldn't have equal rights. In 2008, despite taking great strides in equality, it saddens me to think that a gay or lesbian couple still can't walk down the street without thinking about how their every move is perceived – without being "gawked" and pointed at by passerbyes, says Fletcher.

"And to me that's just wrong!"

And with foreclosures and housing inventory at an all time high, compounded by a sharp decline in consumer spending, many gay and lesbians who need, or want to sell their home, are again getting the short end of the stick – and are at risk of losing thousands of dollars – but there is a solution, as many in the LGBT community have already discovered.

Ryan runs what he calls a "gay-and-lesbian-friendly-outfit" that specializes exclusively in helping Vancouver's LGBT community to increase their home sale profits. According to Fletcher, it's his way of giving back to a community that for far too long has been treated unfairly.

He explains he was inspired to create the LGBT Only Program™ after recently discovering his good friend was gay, and hearing the personal trials-and-tribulations that he's had to endure.

"It's illegal to discriminate against the LGBT community – but unfortunately, that doesn't stop some people!"

Fletcher says "Just the other day, I read a study that reported – one in five lesbian and gay people have been victims of homophobic aggression – ranging from verbal harassment to being physically injured."

"Maybe I was naïve, I don't know, says Ryan. But I never realized just how big of problem this really is."

Fletcher has a point. In recent years, despite an unparalleled effort of social activism from previous years – gay and lesbians in a gay marriage, or civil union, receive only a fraction of the benefits that straight couples enjoy.

Ryan says, "Since, learning these issues – and really understanding them – it's been my personal mission to change mindsets. And provide the LGBT community with real estate services in an environment where they can be treated with the respect they deserve" he says colorfully.

"No hostilities, no judgments, and no "guilt-trip" just for being gay or lesbian."

He continues, "That's why I created the LGBT Only Program™ and why it's offered exclusively to the gay and lesbian community!

Fletcher is the real deal. Before agreeing to write this article, I did my homework. After all, the real estate community hasn't exactly earned the most trustworthy reputation.

Too good to be true?

Nope. Ryan checked out and passed with flying colors. And his past clients seem to love him. In fact, one elderly lady told me, "If she didn't already have 17 grandchildren she'd adopt Ryan as her own!"

Fletcher says, "I don't blame people for being skeptical, that's human nature. But the LGBT Only Program™ has been so successful because it fixed everything that was wrong."

Ryan has been criticized by other agents, brokers, and even the association for his "outside-the-box" style of effective advertising, but claims, "I don't care. I created this program to provide this all too often discriminated-against community with a competitive edge in today's struggling real estate market. So I don't mind if I have to step on a few (political) toes to make that happen!"

Fletcher is a real "hands on guy" dedicated to helping Vancouver gay and lesbian homeowners generate more profits from the sale of their home -- plain and simple!

If you, or someone you know is interested in learning more about the LGBT Only Program™ Ryan has been kind enough to create a free 18-page Special Report titled, **How Vancouver's LGBT Community Can Simply & Easily Discover The Hidden Profits Buried In Their Home Sale!** Ryan explains, by putting every detail into a Free Report, people can enjoy a pressure free environment (in their own home) while they study the specifics, see the proof, determine if they qualify, and ultimately make up their own decision whether or not this program is right for them." This is your opportunity to do all your research first, become an educated consumer, and then decide.

You can claim your FREE copy by visiting the special website setup at ▓▓▓▓▓▓▓▓▓▓ through Ryan's 24-hour toll-free hotline at 1-800-▓▓▓▓▓▓▓ by simply leaving your name and mailing address to ensure fastest delivery – and don't worry, no one will ever call.

And as a special gift for reading this article – Ryan reminds me – you can enter code ▓▓▓▓ receive a special bonus report and gift (offered only to Vancouver's LGBT community).

If you don't think Ryan can help you, just visit the above website, read the testimonials – and please know, you can get the very same help!"

Fletcher is a life-long Vancouver resident, a financial supporter of the VSD, volunteers at SW Medical Center, and is a member of the Chamber of Commerce. His mom teaches a parenting class at Clark College, and he lives locally (in Hazel Dell) with his wife Melanie and many "Lola"!

FIGURE 1-3: Niche Nurses Ad

"New Program Helps Vancouver Nurses Find Hidden Profits Buried In Their Home Sale!"

By Amber Reneau / staff writer

In an industry dominated by negative public perception – where realtors are often referred to as under-trained and over-paid – one local realtor has been strong advocate against what he calls a flawed system, and now, is helping Vancouver nurses escape the real estate "rat race" once and for all.

His name is Ryan Fletcher of Keller Williams Realty – and is the creator of the Nurse Only Program™.

"The Nurse Only Program is not for lawyers, doctors, plumbers, carpet cleaners, or any other profession!"

"People take nurses for granted, not understanding what they have to deal with on a daily basis – working 16 hour days, dealing with egos, and never being treated as equals – truth is, if it weren't for nurses, the entire medical profession would collapse. Yet, most doctors' think it's a nurse's job to chase the chart and follow orders, says Fletcher."

"And to me that's just wrong!"

And with foreclosures and housing inventory at an all time high, compounded by a sharp decline in consumer spending, many nurses who need, or want to sell their home are again getting the short end of the stick – and are at risk of losing thousands of dollars – but there is a solution, as many nurses have already discovered.

Ryan runs what he calls a "nurse-friendly-outfit" and specializes in helping Vancouver-area nurses increase their profits from the sale of their home. It's his way of giving back to a community that has not been properly rewarded for their hard-work and commitment – as public servants.

He explains, he was inspired to create the Nurse Only Program™ after spending several months as an ER volunteer. And seeing first hand, exactly, what nurse's had to put up with on a daily basis.

"The 16-hour days (alone) would kill most people...not to mention, the millions of things nurses do and never get credit for."

"From receptionist, to triage, public relations, medical care, motivational speaker, and social services – there isn't anything that a nurse can't do. And while everyone always comments on how well nurses are paid, very few take into consideration the vast number of overtime hours necessary to make that kind of money, says Fletcher."

He continues, "Despite their importance, and while I'm ashamed to say this, very few doctors really give nurses the respect they deserve. There are still physicians that think nurses should be wearing white tights and a hat, or think nurses should vacate their chair so they can sit. It's disgusting, especially, when you consider it's typically the nurse's rapport with the patient and family that keeps medical mistakes from progressing to lawsuits – and the physician out of hot water.

But this is the reality nurses must endure, day in and day out!"

With more than 30,000 deaths each year, from medical accidents, and prescription drug mistakes – nurses are the ones who often take the brunt of the blame. But as Fletcher explained to me, nurses are blameless victims of a flawed system. They're expected to read illegible handwriting, and when a double check is needed – they're often faced with an attitude of superiority, rude or dismissive actions, even scorned by doctors for "wasting" their time.

"Nurses don't deserve to be treated this way – they deserve something special – to be honored, for their hard work and dedication!"

He continues, "That's why I take created the Nurse Only Program™ and why it's offered exclusively to nurses!

Fletcher is the real deal. Before agreeing to write this article, I did my homework. After all, the real estate community hasn't exactly earned the most trustworthy reputation.

Too good to be true?

Nope. Ryan checked out and passed with flying colors. And his past clients seem to love him. In fact, one elderly lady told me, "If she didn't already have 17 grandchildren she'd adopt Ryan as her own!"

Fletcher says, "I don't blame people for being skeptical, that's human nature. But the Nurse Only Program™ has been so successful because it fixed everything that was missing."

Ryan has been criticized by other agents, brokers, and even the association for his "outside-the-box" style of effective advertising, but claims, "I don't care. I created this program to provide our hard-working and all too often under-appreciated nurses with a competitive edge in today's struggling real estate market. So I don't mind if I have to step on a few (political) toes to make that happen!"

Fletcher is a real "hands on guy" dedicated to helping our nurses generate more profits from the sale of their home – plain and simple!

If you, or a nurse you know is interested in learning more about the Nurse Only Program™ Ryan has been kind enough to create a Free Special Report titled, *How Vancouver Nurses Can Simply & Easily Discover The Hidden Profits Buried In Your Home Sale!*

Ryan explains, by putting every detail into a Free Report, nurses can enjoy a pressure free environment (in their own home) while they study the specifics, see the proof, determine if they qualify, and ultimately make up their own decision whether or not this program is right for them.

You can claim your FREE copy by visiting the special website Ryan setup at ████████████████ or through Ryan's 24-hour nurse hotline at ███████ ███████ by simply leaving your name and mailing address – and don't worry, no one will ever call.

And as a special gift for reading this article – Ryan reminds me – you can enter code ████ to receive a special bonus report and gift (offered only to Vancouver nurses.)

If you don't think Ryan can help you, just visit the above website, read the testimonials – and please know, you can get the very same help!"

Fletcher is a life-long Vancouver resident, a financial supporter of the VSD, volunteers at SW Medical Center, and is a member of the Chamber of Commerce. His mom teaches a parenting class at Clark College, and he lives locally (in Hazel Dell) with his wife Melanie and puppy "Lola"!

FIGURE 1-4: Niche Police Ad

"New Program Helps Vancouver Police Officers Find Hidden Profits Buried In Their Home Sale!"

By Amber Reneau / staff writer

In an industry dominated by negative public perception – where realtors are often referred to as under-trained and over-paid – one local realtor has been strong advocate against what he calls a flawed system, and now, is helping Vancouver police officers escape the real estate "rat race" once and for all.

His name is Ryan Fletcher of Keller Williams Realty – and is the creator of the Officer Only Program™.

"The Officer Only Program is not for lawyers, doctors, plumbers, carpet cleaners, or any other profession!"

"People take cops for granted, not understanding what they have to deal with on a daily basis – both physically and emotionally – knowing that each morning could be their last. Still, people don't like cops – that is, until they need them, says Fletcher."

"And to me that's just wrong!"

And with foreclosures and housing inventory at an all time high, compounded by a sharp decline in consumer spending, many officers who need, or want to sell their home are at risk of losing thousands of dollars – but there is a solution, as many police-officers have already discovered.

Ryan runs what he calls an "officer-friendly-outfit" and specializes in helping Vancouver-area police officers increase their profits (from the sale of their home) as his way of giving back those who have not been properly rewarded for their hard-work and commitment – as a public servant.

He explains he was inspired to create the Officer Only Program™ after hearing many of the grueling cop stories that his long time friend has had to endure.

"You never know when a routine traffic stop is going to turn deadly…or when a unsuspecting 12-year old is going to pull a knife!"

"I never realized the many sacrifices police officers make in their personal life, for the job. Constantly going into drug houses, dealing with people who don't care about life (or "at least" not yours), not to mention the psychological burdens they face from seeing every crime, crash, and unfortunate event – the ones most Americans hope they'll never experience, says Fletcher emphatically"

According to a recent study by a Police Dynamics Institute – cops are 70% more likely to get divorced, twice as likely to abuse alcohol, and three times more likely to commit suicide than the average person.

Cops are addicted to their job, it's a lifestyle and one they must make great sacrifices for – so we "normal" people can live safer, happier lives.

"Seems to me, cops deserve something special – to be honored, not hated!"

"So do the families of our police officers – as I can only imagine what it must be like to kiss your loved one good-bye each morning, knowing it may be the final time – that they may not come home at the end of the day, and that their kids, could very well lose a parent, states Fletcher"

He continues, "That's why I take created the Officer Only Program™ and why it's offered exclusively to cops!

"What's more…the Officer Only Program™ helps raise money for cops injured in the line of duty!"

Not only does Ryan help cops increase their profits from the sale of their home – he also donates $500 to the department for each home he sells through this specialized program.

Fletcher is the real deal. Before agreeing to write this article, I did my homework. After all, the real estate community hasn't exactly earned the most trustworthy reputation.

Too good to be true?

Nope. Ryan checked out and passed with flying colors. And his past clients seem to love him. In fact, one elderly lady told me, "If she didn't already have 17 grandchildren she'd adopt Ryan as her own!"

Fletcher says, "I don't blame people for being skeptical, that's human nature. But the Officer Only Program™ has been so successful because it fixed everything that was missing."

Ryan has been criticized by other agents, brokers, and even the association for his "outside-the-box" style of effective advertising, but claims, "I don't care. I created this program to provide our hard-working and all too often under-appreciated cops with a competitive edge in today's struggling real estate market. So I don't mind if I have to step on a few (political) toes to make that happen!"

Fletcher is a real "hands on guy" dedicated to helping our officers generate more profits from the sale of their home -- plain and simple!

If you, or a cop you know is interested in learning more about the Officer Only Program™ Ryan has been kind enough to create a Free 18-Page Report titled, **How You Can Simply & Easily Discover The Hidden Profits Buried In Your Home Sale!**

Ryan explains, by putting every detail into a Free Report, police-officers can enjoy a pressure free environment (in their own home) while they study the specifics, see the proof, determine if they qualify, and ultimately make up their own decision whether or not this program is right for them."

You can claim your FREE copy by visiting Ryan's website at ▊▊▊▊▊▊▊▊▊▊▊▊▊▊ or through Ryan's 24-hour officer hotline at ▊▊▊▊▊▊▊▊▊▊▊▊ by simply leaving your name and mailing address – and don't worry, no one will ever call.

And as a special gift for reading this article – Ryan reminds me – you can enter code ▊▊▊▊ to receive a special bonus report and gift (offered only to Vancouver police officers.)

If you don't think Ryan can help you, just visit the above website, read the testimonials – and please know, you can get the very same help!"

Fletcher is a life-long Vancouver resident, a financial supporter of the VSD, volunteers at SW Medical Center, and is a member of the Chamber of Commerce. His mom teaches a parenting class at Clark College, and he lives locally (in Hazel Dell) with his wife Melanie and puppy "Lola"!

FIGURE 1-5: Niche Fireman Ad

"New Program Helps Vancouver Firefighters Find Hidden Profits Buried In Their Home Sale!"

By Amber Reneau / staff writer

In an industry dominated by negative public perception – where realtors are often referred to as under-trained and over-paid – one local realtor has been strong advocate against what he calls a flawed system, and now, is helping Vancouver firefighters escape the real estate "rat race" once and for all.

His name is Ryan Fletcher of Keller Williams Realty – and is the creator of the Fireman Only Program™.

"The Fireman Only Program™ is not for lawyers, doctors, plumbers, carpet cleaners, or any other profession!"

"People are always saying how "easy" firefighters have it – how they only work 10 days a month, play basketball, videogames, and so on," says Fletcher. But what most block out – or fail to understand about firefighters – is the physical, emotional, and mental drain of waking up at three in the morning, searching burning buildings, and the vast amount of tragedy they're forced to experience on a daily basis," explains Ryan.

"Sure, being a firefighter is a great job, but it's NO walk in the park!"

Fletcher says firefighters (like cops) and other public servants – are real life heroes. "This isn't just some job people get into for the money. And why they'll never complain – our firemen aren't being paid what they deserve – not for risking their life, and putting their own family's well being in harm's way," he says.

"And when they're not busting their hump for the community – they're working side-jobs for extra cash."

And with foreclosures (and housing inventory) at an all time high, compounded by a sharp decline in consumer spending, many firemen who need (or want) to sell their home are at risk of losing thousands of dollars – but there is a solution, as many have already discovered.

Ryan runs what he calls a "firefighter-friendly-outfit" and specializes in helping Vancouver-area firemen increase the profit from the sale of their home. Fletcher says, it's his way of giving back to a community of public servants that arguably impacts more lives (each year) than any other.

"Firefighter's personal sacrifices are unparalleled!"

"I never realized the many sacrifices firefighters make (in their personal life) for the job. Constantly risking their health, not to mention the psychological burdens they face from seeing every crime, crash, mishap, and unfortunate event known to man – the ones that most Americans hope they'll never have to experience," says Ryan emphatically.

According to a recent study – firefighters are three times more likely to get divorced, twice as likely to develop cancer, and ten times more likely to die of a heart attack than the average person.

Firefighters are addicted to their job says Fletcher. "It's a lifestyle, and one they must make great sacrifices for – so we "normal" people can live safer, happier lives," he says.

"Seems to me, firefighters deserve something special – to be honored for their heroic contributions!"

"So do the families of our firefighters," says Fletcher. He continues, "As I can only imagine what it must be like to kiss your loved one good-bye each morning knowing it may be the final time – that you may not come home at the end of the day, and that your kids could very well lose a parent," says Ryan.

"That's why I take created the Fireman Only Program™ and why it's offered exclusively to our local firefighters!"

"The Fireman Only Program™ also helps raise money for Firefighters injured on the job!"

Not only does Ryan help firemen increase the profit from their home sale – he also donates $500 to the department for each home he sells through this specialized program.

Fletcher is the real deal. Before agreeing to write this article, I did my homework. After all, the real estate community hasn't exactly earned the most trustworthy reputation.

Too good to be true?

Nope. Ryan checked out and passed with flying colors. And his past clients seem to love him.

"I don't blame people for being skeptical says Fletcher. That's human nature. But the Fireman Only Program™ has been so successful because it fixed everything that was missing."

Ryan has been criticized by other agents, brokers, and even the association for his "outside-the-box" style of effective advertising, but claims, "I don't care. I created this program to provide our hard-working and all too often under-appreciated firefighters with a competitive edge they need in today's struggling real estate market. So I don't mind if I have to step on a few (political) toes to make that happen!"

If you, or a firefighter you know is interested in learning more about Ryan's Fireman Only Program™ he's been kind enough to create a Free 18-Page Report titled, **How You Can Simply & Easily Discover The Hidden Profits Buried In Your Home Sale!**

Ryan explains, by putting every detail into a Free Report, firefighters can enjoy a pressure-free environment (in their own home) while they study the specifics, see the proof, determine if they qualify, and ultimately make their own decision whether (or not) this program is right for them.

You can claim your FREE report by visiting Ryan's website at: ▬▬▬▬▬▬ or through Ryan's 24-hour firefighter hotline at 1-800-▬▬▬▬▬ by simply leaving your name and mailing address – and don't worry, no one will ever call.

And as a special gift for reading this article – Ryan reminds me – you can enter code ▬▬▬ to receive a special bonus report and gift (offered only to Vancouver firefighters.)

Fletcher is a life-long Vancouver resident, a financial supporter of the VFD, volunteers at SW Medical Center, and is a member of the Chamber of Commerce. His mom teaches a parenting class at Clark College, and he lives locally (in Hazel Dell) with his wife Melanie and puppy "Lola"!

FIGURE 1-1: Chris Spivey, a member of the Protector/Social Superhero program, has donated dozens of checks to First Responder-connected charities and foundations.

LEGAL NOTICE:

TRADEMARK OWNERSHIP

TEACHER ONLY PROGRAM®, NURSE ONLY PROGRAM®, MILITARY ONLY PROGRAM®, POLICE ONLY PROGRAM® FIREFIGHTER ONLY PROGRAM®, NICHE ONLY PROGRAM®, NEVER TALK TO ANYONE UNTIL THEY KNOW YOU ARE A SOMEONE® are registered trademarks of Ryan Fletcher, and company, Agent Marketing Syndicate®.

SOURCE OF
DIFFERENTIATION #2
Affinity Connection

By Ryan Fletcher

Birds flock. Animals herd. People tribe. When my wife was pregnant with our first child, Jackson, who is now 4-years old, whenever we'd see another pregnant lady at the store, in a restaurant, at the movies, walking down the street—it didn't matter—by some godly, unexplainable and magnetic force, the two of them were drawn to each other like moths to a flame. This is the power of *affinity*.

Merriam-Webster defines affinity as "a spontaneous or natural liking." But perhaps the best explanation for the power of affinity comes from Kalle Jasn, author of the book *Culture Jam*, who explains the cause of this behavior perfectly, by saying: "The most powerful narcotic is the promise of belonging."

Meaning, if you're an atheist, drink beer and like to watch sports, you are infinitely more comfortable at a Sports Bar on Sunday morning, throwing back a few Heinekens—surrounded by others like you—than you are at Church, among others, not like you, who do not share your same values and beliefs. And visa-versa. Why? – Because one place you "belong", at the other, you do not.

When my wife would see another pregnant woman, and they would see her, instantly, each knew they belonged to the same group. The result, affinity, "a natural and spontaneous liking."

I had a client once who revealed to me that he had fought in Vietnam. He was a wounded veteran and had won a number of various medals and awards. Long story short, he has HUGE affinity with military veterans. He is "one of them." He belongs to their fraternity and they belong to his. In his marketing, in his monthly newsletters, on his website and so forth, there should be stories of his military experiences. There should be stories about the different missions he served, stories about him and his platoon in the jungle. The vivid memories he can still see and remember. About the bullets whizzing by his head, in graphic detail. Stories about the enemy, and about the people he met. Stories about the great friends that he lost, saved, respected. The tough lessons he learned, how they changed his life: good, bad and everything between.

Understand. This is why Melanie, my wife, and every other pregnant woman on earth for nine months, were magnetic to each other. They wanted to "swap stories."

Stories are the *true* currency of our society. They connect people. They bond people.

This reaches back to one of the Core Beliefs, in a different business of mine that I founded with a number of my best students, ENG: Entrepreneurs Networking Group™—that is, effective marketing is effective storytelling.

We as humans have a strong innate desire to connect with others of the same ilk—to belong—it really is a Narcotic. It's why *clicks* exist in school. We are a society of diverse groups. Each person is just looking to find that place where they "fit in" and belong. Bill Glazer, Dan Kennedy's co-founder in the membership business Glazer-Kennedy Insider's Circle (GKIC.com) once said, "The Entrepreneur is the loneliest person on Earth." I don't know if that was an original quote nor does it matter. It is the truth. I'm 32, as of this writing, but before my 30th birthday, I had created 4 different 6-figure businesses. My friends were still living with their parents. I wanted to talk business and success. They wanted to go drinking. Which, by the way, I'm all for going drinking with friends, but I don't want to hear their sob stories about not being able to find a job, when they're not willing to better themselves or learn new skills. Yeah, they got college degrees. *Who gives a shit?* This is the real world! In the real world, as you and I know, degrees aren't worth the paper they're printed on.

Needless to say, as an Entrepreneur I've had to seek out and foster new relationships and make new friends, to be able to discuss business and success. My friends from school, whom I love like brothers, make, on average, $55,000 to $60,000/year. My friends from the entrepreneurial world, whom I also love like brothers, make over 6-figures each year. Most make a multiple 6-figure income and several, more than seven-figures. Truth is, I'm no different than any other human being on Earth. I have affinity, magnetism and a desire to belong to certain groups who share (and are passionate about) my different interests. Since my son was born, I have taken a real interest in comic books. Since he "loves all superheroes" we have embedded ourselves in that culture now too.

I also like Rush Limbaugh, and my guess is if you're familiar with Rush, you just had a reaction. Either *"Hey, so do I,"* or perhaps, a more negative response *"Ugh!* I hate Rush Limbaugh." Again, this is the power of affinity. If you hate Rush Limbaugh then you probably love Barack Obama, and have affinity, "a spontaneous or natural liking" with others who also love Obama and Obama policies.

Failure to harness this innate desire "to belong" is just plain stupid.

I am a staunch critic of the typical and foolish ways most real estate agents market and advertise their business: "My ad is bigger than yours"-type stuff. That kind of chest beating with gorilla-like intensity is best reserved for cavemen. Stupid people. Not to be emulated, certainly not envied. It does not make you magnetic. *Affinity* does.

This differentiation strategy can be applied to every industry or category of business, even clothing brands. If you're a true Entrepreneur you undoubtedly watch the hit show on ABC, Shark Tank, where millionaire and billionaire investors like Mark Cuban and Daymond John—founder of the clothing line *FUBU*—compete to invest in entrepreneurs' businesses. It is a great show and you should be watching it if you're not. But going back to *FUBU*, commonly referred to as *For Us By Us,* is a clothing company specializing in African American apparel. Daymond John was born in Brooklyn, grew up in the Hollis neighborhood of Queens. In an article I read, FUBU insists their clothing is not intentionally exclusive to African Americans (Hey, everyone has to be politically correct these days) but you don't see the company advertising in "rich white suburbs." They do not have affinity with that demographic or psychographic.

Daymond John is smarter than that. *FUBU* markets to city youth, in high-density African American populations. That is not a racist thing. It is just smart marketing. Daymond John has *affinity* here. To this group of people, he has a story to tell. The *FUBU* brand has sold over $6 billion dollars of product and merchandize. John started the company by mortgaging his house, as seed money, and since, has followed a very simple formula for success:

Good product + good marketing + AFFINITY = Tribe of loyal customers and clients.

One of the most interesting ways I've seen this strategy used, is in the banking industry with the bank, RedneckBank.com. Yes, that is a real bank. But really, it is just a great marketing strategy to invoke the power of *affinity*.

As it states in the fine print on their website:

"Redneck Bank® is the Internet Banking Division of Bank of the Wichitas®, a bank that was established in 1913, is insured by the FDIC, and has a long history of excellence in the banking industry. So while we have a little fun banking together, you can rest assured your money is safe with us!"

In other words, the real bank is a *generalist* no different than any other big bank, like Chase® or Bank of America®. But which bank do you think a *Redneck (in Oklahoma)* is more likely to patronize and be loyal to as a customer? Redneck Bank® or Bank of America®?

Or what about the dating site, FarmersOnly.com, a dating site exclusively for single farmers. If I'm a farmer and live a unique lifestyle, which site am I more like to feel "at home" on, FarmersOnly.com or Match.com?

Of course, it's a no-brainer. That's what you want. For it to be a no-brainer, because of affinity "a spontaneous or natural liking" to you, your business, your product or service, or who you are and what you stand for.

Earning trust and building relationship is much easier with those, for whom you've walked a mile in their shoes. The question is, who is your ideal client (riches in niches, Differentiation Strategy #1) and what *affinity* do you have with that niche that can be used to your advantage? If you were to look at any of my members' real estate business, you'd notice the creation of a specialized Niche Only Program®, really no different than what the Bank of the Wichitas® has done with RedneckBank.com—a version of their generalized services, customized and specialized to suit a target group of people.

One caveat: You can't fake *affinity*. It has to be real *and* authentic.

So don't try.

When I was an agent, my Niche Only Program® was not operated as a gimmick or marketing ploy. But rather, a deep-seated desire I had to give back to those communities of heroes I chose to serve i.e. military veterans, nurses, teachers, etc.

The proper use of *affinity* is about speaking the *fraternal* language of a certain group. If you take the time to study all the content I produce, in my videos, in my reports, in this book, on my podcast and in my trainings, on my website, etc., AgentMarketingSyndicate.com, you will find a language that resonates with a certain type of agents and repels others. *This is by design.*

Whenever I write copy for clients and seek to pull clients from a group that I, personally, am not familiar with—I spend countless hours researching that group. Who are they? Where do they live? I want to know how they think. I want to know what they believe. What keeps them up at night? What are their fears? Worries? And concerns? I also want to know the kinds of conversations they have, not just publicly, but also, privately. I want to know the conversations they're having in their head, but never talk about out-loud. This is where the power lies in your marketing. The ability to connect with people in ways no one else can, because no one else understands them as you do.

Success, for my clients, and in my own business, and for you in your business, requires that we "ring true" and sound like "one of them," even if we're not. Affinity, sometimes, must be manufactured. But this can only be done if you're able to speak *their* language. So first and foremost, you must strive to get in their heads, to understand the ways they make decisions, and the choices that guide their lives.

It is an undeniable fact: People do business with people, and *patronize* businesses that they know, like and trust.

Affinity is a pathway to achieving all three – it instantly differentiates you from competitors. Any agent or entrepreneur not currently implementing *affinity* in their business "a spontaneous or natural liking" is missing a massive opportunity to *really* connect with their customers and clients. End result: Lost profits. Decreased referrals. Lack of client trust and loyalty and, of course, continued struggle.

Nothing in business comes easy, it seems, until you master this principle of *affinity* connection. Once you do, you're able to harness the world's most powerful narcotic: The promise of belonging.

This changes everything.

Relevant Podcast Episodes: 2, 74, 89, 93

<u>Recommended Resources:</u>

• **Protector Videos Series** (Access inside Member Site)

• **Case Study Interviews** (Access inside Member Site)

• **AMS Podcast** (www.AMSpodcast.com)

• **Forging Elite Storytellers** (www.StoryAthlete.com)

• **90-Day Immersion** (www.90DayImmersion.com)

• **Explore ImpactClub®** (www.ImpactClub.com)

FIGURE 2-1: Affinity-based (niche) website vs. Standard real estate website

Litmus Test: To a fireman, which website (above or below) represents "a spontaneous or natural liking?"

THREE

SOURCE OF
DIFFERENTIATION #3
Names Matter

By Ryan Fletcher

Names matter a lot. Email addresses matter a lot. The website URLs you choose matter a lot. When it comes to positioning, *congruency* is a big deal. One of my businesses is, as I mentioned, Agent Marketing Syndicate.com. I am a big fan of a three part-naming scheme. Agent. Marketing. Syndicate. Another example, ENG: Entrepreneurs Networking Group™. I have also founded and trademarked the term, Niche Only Program®—a positioning concept that I teach to real estate agents, to apply to their businesses to defeat Mega-agents.

So why is this important? Why do these names matter?

For a minute, let's go back in time. Let's say I was a real estate agent again, as I was in my past business life. My positioning might sound like this, Ryan Fletcher, Founder & CEO of the Military Only Program® can be reached at: Ryan@MilitaryOnlyProgram.com or online at MilitaryOnlyProgram.com. Now, if I'm reaching out to military veterans as my target market, common sense tells you this kind of positioning is infinitely more powerful than "John Smith Home Selling Team," reached at: John@JohnSellsHomes.com or online at: www.JohnSellsHomes.com. *Why?* Because one is *WHO*-focused, the other is *YOU*-focused.

WHO*-focused, means focused on the prospective client. *YOU*-focused, means focused on you, the service provider. Hopefully, you can see how the latter is ego-driven. While the first, is *affinity*-driven.

I give you this Niche Only Program® naming concept, merely as an example. It was not hastily thrown together, it is a positioning statement in just three words: Niche. Only. Program. Said differently, the name of the program, 1) Calls out to target market, 2) Creates exclusivity, and 3) Offers the targeted group, whatever the chosen niche is, access to a special program.

I submit to you: It is not always possible to put a positioning statement into the name of your business, or, the special programs you create, but it is a powerful strategy if it can be done. In differentiation strategy #2, you saw a brilliant example of this, *FUBU*, For Us By Us. Here, also, it has been applied to ENG: Entrepreneurs Networking Group™. If someone heard nothing else but its name, it would be clear to them *who* we are, *what* we do, and the type of people we benefit i.e. entrepreneurs.

Names of Free Reports, free books, free information packages, etc. for lead generating offers are important too.

Consider the name of the manuscript used by P/SS members and myself to generate leads for Entrepreneurs Networking Group™, which, as an aside, is a modified version of this book—in a condensed report format. ENG, by the way, opened 28 chapters in its first week, on two continents, making it the fastest growing networking group of its kind. But, I digress. Back to the name of the

manuscript, "14 Marketing and Positioning Gamechangers For Any Business Owner, Sales Professional and Entrepreneur to Increase Profits & Give More Back."

Based on the name [of this book] alone, who do you imagine is most likely to respond to our offer and request access to this publication? Of course, business owners, sales professionals and entrepreneurs who want to increase their profits, and, who want to impact their communities by giving more back.

The point is: Names, what you name your business, your programs, your Free Reports, what you use as your email address, your website address, etc.—they all matter. Congruency, between each of those names, that matters too. You don't want to offer a Military Only Program™, for example, and then send people to the website www.JohnSellsHomes.com. That is piss poor. But sadly, most agents are negligent about these kinds of *positioning* decisions and it's a shame.

When I see an agent using a gmail.com account, or comcast.net account, or an aol or yahoo.com account for his email address, I cringe in terror. Too many agents and entrepreneurs are guilty of this. By simply changing my email, for example, from fletcher56@gmail.com to Ryan@AgentMarketingSyndicate.com I elevate my status as a business owner. I have also invoked the power of *names*.

Just look back to RedneckBank.com. It's the strategic choice of that *name* that creates the *affinity*. Why would you not want to include it everywhere possible? Obviously, and yes, making it the email address, JohnDoe@RedneckBank.com, for all bank employees and any of its representatives.

This might seem like a small and insignificant detail, but I can't count how many times I have visited someone's website because I saw their URL in their email address. And those URL's that invoke affinity, "a natural and spontaneous liking," get visited more often. For this reason, I have many different email addresses; Ryan@AgentMarketingSyndicate.com, @DefeatMegaAgents.com, @EntrepreneursNetworkingGroup.com, etc. and I use, in my marketing, whatever email address I think will best resonate with the avatar that is trying to be reached.

So simple, yet a positioning opportunity squandered by many.

Relevant Podcast Episodes: 19, 36

<u>Recommended Resources:</u>

• **Protector Videos Series** (Access inside Member Site)

• **Case Study Interviews** (Access inside Member Site)

• **AMS Podcast** (www.AMSpodcast.com)

- **Value-Driven Approach** (www.TheValueDrivenApproach.com)

- **Forging Elite Storytellers** (www.StoryAthlete.com)

- **90-Day Immersion** (www.90DayImmersion.com)

- **Explore ImpactClub®** (www.ImpactClub.com)

SOURCE OF
DIFFERENTIATION #4
Proprietary Secret

By Ryan Fletcher

S ecrets *trump* information. There was a famous marketer by the name of Marty Edelston, the creative brain and "Man Of A Million Interests" behind Boardroom Inc. (founded in 1971), the juggernaut publisher of newsletters like *Bottomline/Health* and *Bottomline/Business* and direct-to-consumer book publishing mega-hits like *The 30-Day Diabetes Cure* and other health books. Although Marty recently died, his fabulous creation and unique direct-mail approach continues to be copied by smart marketers. Marty built a $50 million dollar business on the premise that almost everybody secretly, if not openly, believes in secrets, wants to believe in secrets, and are eager to believe that one or a few secrets—perhaps withheld from them by conspiracy—are all that stand between them and their particular aspiration.

Should you need to prove it to yourself, the power of secrets, consider most people's response to being told that you have a secret.

Their response, "What is it? C'mon. Tell me!" to which you say, "Nah, it's nothing." But they persist, "Just tell me. I'm not going to say anything." And, if you continue to resist, they begin plotting ways to get you to squeal. They usually get mad. Then they devise their own secret out of thin air, "Fine! I'm not telling you what I know" to which you ask, "What do you know?" And they respond, "First tell me what you know, then I'll tell you the secret I know."

Take note: if you're NOT the *keeper* of "secrets", inherently, you are a lot less interesting and magnetic to prospective clients.

Most business owners, marketers, and sales professionals seek only to educate their clients, i.e. provide *information*, when, in fact, they should be positioning themselves as the *keeper* of secrets. Secrets that *could* deliver a prospective client their ideal outcome! Secrets that *could* eliminate a prospective client's pain and suffering! Secrets that *could* differentiate you, the business owner, the agent, from all competition, because you possess the secret (the client wants) and your competition does not!

Do you know how hard it is to find the 3 secret strategies I used to generate $571,856.89 for a client in just 5 hours and 43 minutes? And yes, I really did that. And yes, I used only three key strategies that any business owner, sales professional or entrepreneur,

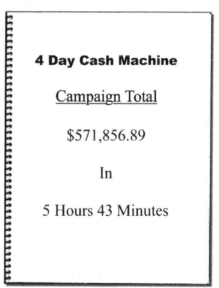

4 Day Cash Machine

<u>Campaign Total</u>

$571,856.89

In

5 Hours 43 Minutes

including any real estate agent, could use to generate a similar flood of cash. But, do you know what those three secret strategies are? Do you know where to look or how to find them? I suppose, you could try to guess. Maybe you could attempt to Google them. *Oh wait.* No, you can't. *Why?* Because they're *secret* strategies! If you were going to type something into Google, what would you even type?

Secrets are not readily available. Information is. Secrets *are* not. Secrets are *rare* and valuable. *Hard to find...*

Understand we're dealing with perception here. People want to believe there's a secret out there that is being kept from them and, that if, they just knew this secret, their lives would improve almost instantly. They could be: Skinnier. Richer. Happier. Healthier. Grow their business to a new record level. The stress and frustration, the sleepless nights, for example, of not getting enough good clients each month, could be eliminated. This is, by the way, how I sell my consulting services—I position myself as the *keeper* of certain secrets pertaining to business, profit and growth strategies.

Listen closely: If prospective (real estate) clients perceive you to be the *keeper* of such secrets, secrets relevant to them and their needs; their wants, desires, able to solve their problems, end their worries and fears, and eliminate their frustration. And, you position yourself as the *keeper* of these secrets—known by you, only by you, and no one else—hence, *proprietary*—you will be sought out by prospective clients.

Defeating Mega-agents will not be a problem for you.

This makes the *task* of "how" you position your knowledge and expertise and, your real estate services, of critical importance.

Your competitor, and you, likely, share the same fundamental knowledge about real estate. But how you choose to position that knowledge; information vs. the *keeper* of secrets, creates vastly different perceptions about each of your unique abilities. Hint: Magicians never have a hard time attracting a crowd. They possess secrets. Just look at David Blaine and Criss Angel.

Secondly, proprietary secrets positioned as: Secret formulas, Secret systems, Secret technologies, processes, etc., can, and should be, a deliberate form of differentiation in your real estate business.

When you claim to be able to achieve superior results for a client, the first objection in that prospective client's head is: "How are you able to do that? How is that possible? How are you able to achieve what you say you're able to achieve?"

What he is really asking is, "What's your secret?"

Certainly you've heard of Proactiv, America's #1 Acne Treatment. When teens and adults with acne are told of Proactiv's ability to eliminate acne, their first thought is, "I've heard that before. How is this product any different than all the others I've tried?" Answer: The *secret* is Proactiv's New, Micro-Crystal Benzoyl Peroxide Formula. The benzoyl-peroxide particles in New Proactiv are now many times smaller. The New micro-crystals are designed to penetrate the pores fast and start killing acne on contact. It works within the skin, not just on the surface. *That's the secret!*

Or how about the promise of P90X, the best-selling fitness program? When folks are told they can shed pounds, get ripped and be in the best shape of their lives in just 90 days, their first thought is, "Bullshit! How is this any different than the other 40 infomercials all promising the same ridiculous outcome?" Answer: The Science of Muscle Confusion™. Here's the true *secret* of how P90X works: Muscle Confusion. P90X uses targeted training phases so your body keeps adapting and growing. You'll never "plateau" – which means your body will never get used to the routines, making improvements slow down or even stop.

Hell even Colonel Sanders has his KFC *Secret* Recipe: 11 Secret Herbs and Spices. Or how about Coca Cola? Their *secret* ingredient, cryptically dubbed "Merchandise 7X" has remained secret since the sodas invention in 1886. Coke has kept its prized "list of ingredients" in a vault inside the Trust Company Bank since 1925 and goes to extreme lengths to keep their *proprietary* secret, secret.

Then there's eHarmony®. They don't just match people. People are matched using a proprietary Compatibility Matching System®, which matches men and women on 29 Dimensions® of Compatibility for lasting and fulfilling relationships. They claim this is the *secret*, why match.com is responsible for more marriages than any other dating site.

Every real estate agent and entrepreneur should ask the question: "What is my (secret) *Proprietary* System, Process, Formula, Technology, or otherwise, for achieving superior client results?"

I will tell you as firmly as I can: Ignore this question at your extreme peril. For many years in business, I didn't take this question seriously. I simply didn't know how critical it was. And what you don't know, well, you don't know. But now I do know, and I'm telling you: Proprietary secret(s) differentiate you.

It doesn't matter if you're a service-provider, retailer, restaurateur, etc. or when you have one product or hundreds of products for sale; your product, your service should differentiate itself from others (in its product category or industry of business) by possession of a secret system, process, formula, ingredient, technology or otherwise, that can explain the superior results that you're able to get for your clients.

For members of my Agent Marketing Syndicate® business, together, we created and pioneered a method of selling real estate known as: "The Value-Driven Approach to Sell Real Estate." I have also written a book on this approach that members can *license* for exclusive use, as a co-author, in their geographic market area.

When speaking to a client, they say:

> "We have seen the traditional approach to real estate disappoint many of our clients. This is why we've studied the World's greatest investor, Warren Buffet, and his investment philosophy to develop a unique approach to selling our clients homes. We've discovered, by treating your home as an investment—like a business with a "stock" price—there is a unique way to extract up to $30,000 or more of additional profit from any home on the market."

Of course, there is a lot more to this approach than described here. But this statement, as you can see, helps to position P/SS members as: the *Keeper of Secrets*.

Question to ask: In the eyes of your prospective clients, are you positioned and seen as, the *Keeper of Secrets?*

If not, this presents an opportunity to increase the effectiveness of your positioning; to become more fascinating to those that you seek to do business with. Be the *Magician*, and you shall always have an audience for which you can sell your goods and services.

Also, it is one of the keys to defeat Mega-agents. If you can't beat them on marketing budget, you must beat them with mystique and intrigue.

Relevant Podcast Episodes: 2, 26, 31, 43, 44, 51-54, 75-78

<u>Recommended Resources:</u>

• **Protector Videos Series** (Access inside Member Site)

• **Case Study Interviews** (Access inside Member Site)

• **AMS Podcast** (www.AMSpodcast.com)

• **Value-Driven Approach** (www.TheValueDrivenApproach.com)

• **Forging Elite Storytellers** (www.StoryAthlete.com)

• **90-Day Immersion** (www.90DayImmersion.com)

• **Explore ImpactClub®** (www.ImpactClub.com)

FIVE

SOURCE OF

SOURCE OF
DIFFERENTIATION #5
Added Value

By Ryan Fletcher

I 'll never forget the Christmas three years ago. It was early December or so, Melanie and I are lying in bed, she looks out the window, the sun is out, and its absolutely beautiful outside. She turns to me and decides, "Today is the day we get the tree!" So I loaded up the family. I grabbed the stroller, the straps and tie-downs, and now we're driving to the tree farm.

When I lived in Florida for a few years, Delray Beach area, you didn't bother going to cut down a Christmas tree. You just stopped roadside, grabbed the tree that was the least brown, least brittle, least ugly, and that was that.

At home in Vancouver, Washington, though, a much different story. You have options. There's a tree farm on every corner and on every intersection, usually two or three. So Melanie chooses the place. En route to getting there, we pass about 25 other tree farms. Almost all of them were empty. Fifteen miles later, the one she chose is packed. Cars are spilling out of the parking lot into the street. I had to pay to park. By the time I parked and walked to the trees, I was two miles from my car. I had to wait in line 30 minutes to pay. The 10-foot Noble I purchased, was $20 more than every tree advertised at every tree farm on the way to get to this one. So I say to Melanie, I'm really impatient by the way, "Why the hell did you choose this place?"

She says to me, "They have a petting zoo!" *Huh? A petting zoo?*

At the time, Jackson had just turned one. Melanie had decided that he needed to see the animals. *Period.* She didn't care if the tree farm was more expensive. She didn't care if it was more of a pain-in-the-ass to get to. None of that mattered. She wanted the petting zoo. That's why we were there. Had there not been a petting zoo, we definitely would not have been there. We would have been somewhere else.

Three words: Smart Tree Farmer. (He had a petting zoo).

When your product or service is commoditized, like a Christmas tree, inherently, and intrinsically, no different than any other Christmas tree—at least not to the common man, like me—you must find a way to differentiate.

This tree farmer did it with an "Add-on" to his core product. Normally, there are no animals on his tree farm. But intelligently, knowing he needed to differentiate himself from the cheaper, easier, more convenient to get to tree farms in the area, he went to a nearby friend, rounded-up a few of his goats, threw up some chicken wire as a pen, bought some feed, which was an extra $5 per handful (yes, Jackson *had* to feed the goats) and viola, he had a petting zoo. And, although, this "petting zoo" was not in any way connected to the process of buying a Christmas tree, nor the quality of his trees vs. his competitor's trees, nor did it have anything to do with a better selection of trees—it was a huge attraction.

In fact, it was the *main* attraction.

The Christmas Tree Farmer *also* partnered with a local catering company, providing yet another "add-on" to enhance his customers' experience.

I imagine the conversation went like this: "Mr. Food Truck Owner, I'll tell ya what. I got this petting zoo out here, three goats in a small cage. People are going to love it. People are going to come from miles away. They're going to drive past 47 other tree farms just to get here, just to pet and feed these goats. They're going to pay $5 for three pebbles of goat food too. The parking lot is going to be packed. There will be swarms of people, and, sooner or later they're going to get hungry. So here's the thing. Why don't you come out here, I'll deliver all the customers to the farm. All you have to do is, when they get hungry and come to your food truck, you feed them. You can even keep all the money, fair enough?"

He did the same thing with a half-dozen other business owners too. I imagine he went to the sketch artist with a similar proposition. "Why don't you come out here, draw some families, you can charge whatever you like, you can even keep all the money." Etc.

Long story short, Melanie did NOT plan on getting a tree and coming home. She planned to make a day of it. Buying the Christmas tree was just one of several activities, not the sole focus. Four hours later, I was the proud owner of an *overpriced* tree, enjoyed an *overpriced* corndog, fed some goats with some *overpriced* feed, and had an *overpriced* sketch of the family, with our overpriced tree in the background. This "portrait," by the way, is still paraded out each

Christmas as a memory of that day, and hung on the fridge during the holidays.

This Christmas tree farmer, he didn't look like much. But this old crotchety, 70 to 75-year old tree farmer was extremely savvy. This was not his first rodeo. Unlike his competitors, he was not selling Christmas trees—a commoditized product—he was providing people an EXPERIENCE.

His competitors were all just selling "trees." *TREES!* And to be fair, they probably had nicer tress, a better selection of trees, certainly their trees were better priced, and yet, their parking lots barren by comparison. What was the real secret?

This old Christmas tree farmer understood that buying a Christmas tree isn't about the tree at all. It is about the experience. For Melanie, it was about the three goats positioned as a "petting zoo." By the way, I bet all of his competitors laughed at him for that too. If not out loud, they said to themselves, "Look at that old fool and his "petting zoo," what an idiot!" But look who got the last laugh. A mentor of mine once said to me: "Who laughs first doesn't matter, only who laughs last." I guess this is what he meant.

To defeat Mega-agents, a smart question to ask: What 'Add-On' can you "add on" to your core product-line or menu of services that, in the same way, would have great value and meaning to your prospective client, like that petting zoo did for Melanie, to differ-entiate yourself from competitors?

Like it or not, acknowledge it or not, accept it or not—the public views real estate agents as interchangeable, and are as commoditized as Christmas trees.

With the use of this strategy, though, a little hustle, thought, and ingenuity, a smart agent can transform his *ordinary* set of services, no different than buying a Christmas tree, into an *extraordinary* experience. One that clients will pay more for, travel inconvenient distances for, and tell friends and family members about because they enjoyed themselves.

This is how you defeat Mega-agents with bigger marketing budgets and more resources.

You follow in the footsteps of a crotchety old Christmas tree farmer, and create *added* value.

Relevant Podcast Episodes: 17, 25, 27, 96

<u>Recommended Resources:</u>

• **Protector Videos Series** (Access inside Member Site)

• **Case Study Interviews** (Access inside Member Site)

• **AMS Podcast** (www.AMSpodcast.com)

• **Value-Driven Approach** (www.TheValueDrivenApproach.com)

• **Forging Elite Storytellers** (www.StoryAthlete.com)

• **90-Day Immersion** (www.90DayImmersion.com)

• **Explore ImpactClub®** (www.ImpactClub.com)

DEFEAT MEGA-AGENTS

SIX

SOURCE OF
DIFFERENTIATION #6
Charitable Mission

By Ryan Fletcher

"It's for a good cause!" That is fast becoming most powerful statement in selling. It is a justification statement. It is a guilt statement. It is a movement statement. It is a call to action. It is a mission, of one or more people.

Three years ago, my good friend's dad was diagnosed with a rare form of cancer. He survived. Since, in support, she (my friend) has done more than two-dozen cancer walks. In most cases, she organized a team of no less than 20 or 30 walkers/runners who shared her same passion of "It's for a good cause!" It unites people. And collectively, last I heard, her teammates and her have raised well over $10,000 for cancer research. Prior to her dad being diagnosed, she participated in *only* one.

I'll give you another example. For 31 consecutive years my Mom has donated to the March of Dimes®, for one reason. When my cousin Heather was born, she had a hole in little her heart. My uncle

couldn't afford the surgery she needed, so the March of Dimes®
stepped in and covered 100% of the cost. My cousin didn't make it.
She died before her first birthday. But ever since, there's never been a
year that my Mother hasn't donated to the March of Dimes®. Why?
Because, "It's for a good cause!" My Mom has since branched out to
donate to a number of other similar charities focused on helping
babies and children, from St. Jude's Children's Hospital to Smile
Train® and several others.

You Can't Argue With The Facts.

According to research, when a business is seen as (A) partnering
with, and (B) truly benefiting a non-profit organization or cause,
consumers with some affinity *to that cause* are 59% more likely to
respond or patronize that business than a business without the
attachment (source: Philanthropy, Consumer Spending & Attitudes
Survey, reported by Research Associates). In other words, a business
attempting to sell my friend a product or service, of any kind, is 59%
more likely to be successful, if…in some way, that product or service
is connected to raising money for cancer research, victims or
survivors.

But before you run out and "tack on" a charitable component to
your business. Understand. Your *Charitable Mission* should be sincere.
A fine line exists between mission and *exploitation,* and that line is
genuine authenticity.

In 2006, American traveler Blake Mycoskie, while on a trip in
Argentina was shocked to discover that local children had no shoes
to protect their feet. He wanted to help. Upon returning to the U.S.,
he created TOMS shoes. A company that would match every pair of

shoes purchased, with a pair given to a child in need. One for one. Ever since, Mycoskie has strived to further his movement to raise awareness for children without shoes, officially declaring April 5th, "One Day Without Shoes Day," and encouraging customers to "join" in the Barefoot Challenge.

When I was a pre-med student at Washington State University, I traveled to Africa on a three-month medical mission. I met many of the local children. Amazing kids. Virtually none of these kids had shoes. Their feet were giant calluses. Many of these kid's feet were cracked and bleeding. This posed a huge health risk. One of the leading causes of disease in developing countries is soil-transmitted-diseases. Parasites penetrate the skin through cracks and tears in the feet, ultimately causing diarrhea, and death by dehydration.

An *authentic* Charitable Mission can differentiate you.

TOMS shoes is not just a shoe company, they are, by positioning, a Health & Education Organization too. On their website they brilliantly ask the question, "Why Shoes?" They answer it by saying, "Simple, because 1) Wearing shoes can prevent disease, 2) Wearing shoes prevents cuts and sores that lead to infection, and 3) Without shoes many children aren't allowed to attend school, as shoes are a required part of their uniforms."

In my mind, there is no doubt the TOMS' *Charitable Mission* is authentic. As a result, with an *authentic* charitable mission, TOMS successfully changed the rules of the game—no longer must they compete against traditional shoe companies. While most shoe companies talk about their shoes; a totally commoditized product. TOMS is able to talk about their vision to impact the world. Using their shoes, "It's for a good cause!" as merely the vehicle and catalyst to fulfill their mission.

To get a better understanding of this, I encourage you to visit the company's website www.Toms.com. You'll immediately notice their Mission: "With every pair you purchase, TOMS will give a pair of new shoes to a child in need. One for one." If you click on the tab that says, "Our Movement," you're able to watch the 3-minute documentary of the company's founder, Mycoskie, handing out free pairs of shoes. Watching this, you get the point: An authentic 'Charitable Mission' differentiates you. More important, it attracts to you clients of a certain belief system. When Nike sells a shoe, they gain a customer. When TOMS sells a shoe, they gain a loyal supporter and potential evangelist that are likely to spread the vision of the company far and wide to family and friends. After all, "It's for a good cause."

This is how a company can (deliberately) start a movement.

What is your charitable mission? Is it authentic? Does it resonate with and, also, is it a *passionate* subject of interest to your target market?

For a real estate client of mine, and a member of my Protector/Social Superhero program, this differentiation approach was used to promote her customer appreciation event, but, re-positioned as: Outdoor Movie Night *For Hunger*™.

This landed her on the front page of her local newspaper and, on the inside pages three other times. She also received free publicity via radio and attracted over 30 local businesses to sponsor the event, including globally recognized brands: Mercedes Benz, Lowes, and

Sun-Life Financial. In the end, nearly 2,000 people in her community attended. Over 3,000 lbs. of food was collected for her local food bank. And in no time flat, because of the multiple events "for hunger" that she conducted—each fueled by media exposure; newspaper, radio, virally on social media, and on television—she became very well-known and somewhat of a local "celebrity" in her marketplace.

Do not forget. A real estate agent did this. This just proves that this can be applied to your business too.

In fact, using this same concept of mixing philanthropy and business, another member of mine, Nate Robinson, at the time of this writing, has secured Petco field—home of the San Diego Padres—for a charity event associated with his real estate business and Military Only Program®. In the early promotion, he's already attracted big name sponsors, Allstate and Kinecta Federal Credit Union among others. Secured legendary guitar player, Greg Douglass, former member of the Steve Miller Band and Van Morrison. Has been interviewed on 1700AM ESPN radio and, just recently, locked in their full support as you can read in the update from Nate on the next page:

Nathan Robinson	So i just left ESPN Studios in San Diego and…. It totally Rocked!!! Not only Jul-11 3:09 PM are they going to interview us on the Radio on the Tuesday before our Outdoor Movie Night for Hunger event. They will also interview on the Thursday before the event. Run free airtime blitz for 48 hours prior to the event. In addition they are gathering items to be raffled at the event such as Padres/Chargers tickets, $500 Cash Prize, doo dads, and doo hickeys to be raffled off, connections to the sponsors of the radio show to get them to sponsor our event with a booth. Thank You @CherylGordon for letting me use a few pics from your past events. @DouglasHeron for posting the Cause Marketing article it helps when presenting to the potential sponsors. Thank You @all for giving the way you do. Most Importantly I just want to THANK YOU Ryan for being a great player/coach to us all. I am blown away!!!!! Hide full text

So yes, this is a big time event.

One certain to make Nate a well-known name in his marketplace;

a "celebrity" and a *Someone*. Not to mention, will greatly impact his community and fuel his real estate business as 3,000 to 5,000 people are expected to be in attendance. And due to the fact that Nate has six such events planned throughout the San Diego area—at Qualcomm Stadium too—his status as a local celebrity and as a leader in his community is likely to mushroom.

Nate's mission and goal by December 31st 2015 is to raise 500,000 meals, and donate over $100,000 in cash for non-food related needs, to his local food bank.

Why is this powerful? It's common sense.

People do business with people they know, like and trust. To be liked, you must do *likeable* things. Raising money, awareness and/or giving back to a charitable cause—is about the fastest, easiest, and best way to be liked, that there is.

People trust philanthropists.

An *authentic* Charitable Mission differentiates you. It also virtually guarantees you free publicity and wide spread media exposure. Not to mention, a way to greatly impact your community.

Implementation of this one strategy could change your business forever. It has for Protector/Social Superhero members of mine. By the way, that name—of the program—was chosen for a reason. It is an area that we focus on heavily, becoming *Social* Superheroes!

Relevant Podcast Episodes: 6, 28, 44, 91

<u>Recommended Resources:</u>

• ***Protector Videos Series*** (Access inside Member Site)

• **Case Study Interviews** (Access inside Member Site)

• **AMS Podcast** (www.AMSpodcast.com)

• **Value-Driven Approach** (www.TheValueDrivenApproach.com)

• **Forging Elite Storytellers** (www.StoryAthlete.com)

• **90-Day Immersion** (www.90DayImmersion.com)

• **Explore ImpactClub®** (www.ImpactClub.com)

FIGURE 6-1: Outdoor Movie Night For Hunger™ Ad (Actual size: 11 x 17 Poster)

FIGURE 6-2: Top section of Nate Robinson's Outdoor Movie Night For Hunger™ website—copyright protected/licensed to P/SS members along with all promotional tools, package for sponsorship, etc.—announcing in the video here, that Kinecta Federal Credit Union has become a Platinum Level Sponsor (requiring a $2,500 donation.)

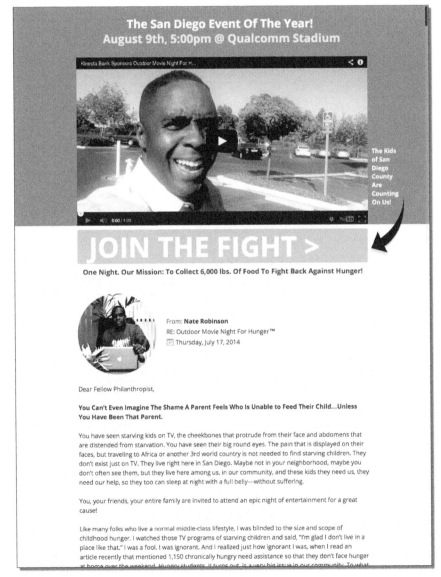

SEVEN

SOURCE OF
DIFFERENTIATION #7
Power of Story

By Ryan Fletcher

How often do people *naturally* talk about you, or gravitate toward you? How much appetite is there for your ideas and opinions? How often does someone refer your services? What kind of response do you *elicit* with your words, actions or ideas? Do you prompt others to think in new ways? How often do others imitate you in their behavior, ideas or techniques?

The most direct path to increase your effectiveness and influence in each of these categories is to become more fascinating. How do you become more fascinating? You tell stories about yourself. About your business. About your products and services. About your customers and clients.

Mark Victor Hansen and his partner Jack Canfield had their book idea "Chicken Soup for The Soul" rejected by over 100 book publishers. These publishers could not see what Mark and Jack knew, and what every copywriter worth their salt must keep in forefront of their mind: nothing captures attention like the power of story. And specifically, nothing engages and connects with people on a deeper level than *human*-interest stories.

Think about the movie 'Rudy', the story of Rudy Ruettiger. Or 'Blindside', which won Sandra Bullock the Oscar for best actress.

Both are human-interest stories.

The same is true about all the books in the "Chicken Soup for the Soul" series. Each book is just a collection of *human*-interest stories. People love them. In fact, this series is so successful, if you visit Amazon.com and search "Chicken Soup for The Soul," you're presented 6,124 different buying options. Even if each of these search results is not unique, I'm certain there are over 1,000 different books titles. Including this one, "Chicken Soup for the Soul: I Can't Believe My Cat Did That!" written to connect and resonate with cat owners.

You must understand, this is a business empire and publishing phenomenon based solely on the tales of random folks. Mark and Jack are the envy of all authors, because they don't even write the content published in their books. Other people write the stories. About their lives, feelings and experiences. Or even their cats.

The premise is drawn from a staple ingredient of the highest circulation, most read publications of all time like *Reader's Digest* and *National Enquirer*. The formula is this: People are fascinated with stories that are written about people they can somehow identify with and relate to. After all, who do you think is the major buyer of the "Chicken Soup for The Soul: I can't Believe My Cat Did That!"

book. You guessed it. *Creepy cat people!* I personally hate cats. I would never buy such a book. But this is why there are a thousand different books in the series. Certainly, one of the titles will resonate with someone like me. Perhaps, "Chicken Soup for the Entrepreneur's Soul: Advice and Inspiration on Fulfilling Dreams." A collection of *human*-interest stories of entrepreneurs as they document their successes and failures.

Most human-interest stories are built on the *framework* of classic Hollywood storylines: Before and after, tragedy and recovery, bravery and heroism, rags to riches, loneliness to romance, dullsville to *living* an exciting life.

My point here: In order for marketing and advertising to be effective, it must grab attention and secure readership. So why not wrap your marketing message in the context of a human-interest story, and on the framework of a classic Hollywood storyline—perhaps, the before and after? What was your client's situation *before* your product or service? What is their situation like now, *after* your product or service? How has their life been improved or transformed? Have their frustrations been eliminated? In what ways have their problems been solved?

Pretty simple to understand, before you, and then after you—how did their life or circumstance change as the result of your product or service? Hopefully, for the better.

Second, to have impact, your marketing message must be remembered.

Using statistics and figures and product descriptions, it is nearly impossible to achieve any lasting affect. People can't even remember where they parked their damn car. They aren't going to remember the mundane details of your product or service. Next time you come out of a movie theatre, just pay attention to the people around you. You will see people wandering about like drunken toddlers. One will be pointing right, their spouse or significant other will point left and, ultimately, whoever has the keys will push the panic button. When the horn honks and lights flash, this is the only way they can find their car.

They just can't remember.

But 37 years later, little Betty, I assure you—now grown-up Betty—remembers the vivid details of being humiliated on the playground in front of her schoolmates like it was yesterday. Why? Because memories are emotions. Kids who grew up in abusive household, years and years later, can still describe how they felt hiding under the stairs, or in a back bedroom, while dad beat mom to a bloody pulp. Why? Because memories are emotions.

If you wish to be remembered, to have a lasting impact on prospects and clients, your marketing message must engage people emotionally. *Stories* do this. Human-interest stories especially.

If you went through my entire archive of copywriting work for myself, in my own business and for private clients, including my real estate agent members, you'd find a vast collection of human-interest stories. For one client, I told the story of his unique background. The headline read: *"Sounds weird, but in Camden you weren't born to do what you loved, like the mining towns of Pennsylvania and steel mills of Pittsburgh, you were born and expected to work at the plant from teenage to grave"...* which then went on to tell how the story of he worked his way to the top of his profession, with no college education, no degrees, no high profile mentors or silver-spoon handouts. In doing this, I wrapped his marketing message into a human-interest story.

Another good example of this is a guy named Darin Garman.

Darin is a commercial real estate broker in Grand Rapids, Iowa. In his advertising, he tells the story of being a poorly paid, depressed Iowa prison guard who, in a prior life bumbled across his first "how-to-succeed" book while cooling his heels in the warden's office. Somehow a beer bottle found its way into the trashcan next to his desk. So while he was waiting for the warden to arrive in his office. He grabbed a book off the shelf. Started reading it, and before the warden could fire him, Darin quit. The next day, he started in real estate and became rich in the following years, applying what he learned in that book. My question, don't you want to know which book that was? Or, how he did it? By the way, last I heard, Darin owns more than $10 million in commercial real estate.

Or how about the young kid who dreamed of going to medical school, but after 47 rejections over a four-year period (from 33 different medical schools) found his way into real estate, where he struggled, was broke, and ended up taking a job as a box-boy at UPS in order to buy Christmas presents for his family. Have you heard the story about this young man? He didn't have much money, so he decided he'd buy his sister a book. She loved books. So on December 11th, 2006, he strolled into a Barnes & Noble. In his wallet was $19.63. That's what he had left from his UPS paycheck. While he searched for the book his sister wanted, he stumbled upon a book that forever changed his life. This book was *The Ultimate Sales Letter* by Dan Kennedy. That book said you could write a letter, mail it, and get clients. "Bullshit," the young man thought to himself. "Another fantasy-tale of 'easy success' in business." He had heard it all before. But for some reason, this time, it was different. *He believed.* Maybe it was the desperation… Maybe it was…

Of course, that story is mine. Within 12 months, after reading that book and discovering direct-response copywriting, and after making only $8,882 my entire first year in real estate, the next year, I made over $180,000 working a fraction of the hours. No cold calling. No prospecting. And all clients came to me.

As they say, the rest is history.

You can read a shortened version of "what's happened since" in Chapter 15 towards the end of the book.

But this is my point. One of the reasons I'm paid handsomely by private clients, for complex, multi-step, multi-media projects; fees that range from $25,000 to $50,000 plus royalties tied to results, is for my ability to unearth and tell *these stories*, and use them in such a context that encompasses their marketing message.

Even for the *most* boring business, selling the ultimate commodity, human-interest stories can provide differentiation.

In the 1990's there was a young man. He was a junior in college at the time, and his weight had ballooned to over 425 pounds. His t-shirt was a size 6XL. As you can imagine, not even the big-and-tall stores carried a large enough size. His pants, he had a 60-inch waist. The young man's father was a general practitioner, who, one day told him, given his weight and general health, that he might not live past thirty-five. After an emergency visit to the hospital, the young man decided to slim down. He started eating sandwiches, 6-inch turkey clubs, three times each day. After three months, he had lost almost 100 pounds.

Do you know the rest of this story? Can you name the young man that this story is about? Can you name the "sandwich joint" at which he ate?

Of course you can. Everyone can. Jared and Subway.

The first ad spot ran on January 1st, 2000. It showed Jared in front of his home. "This is Jared", the announcer said. "He used to weigh 425 pounds," as a photo of Jared in his old 60-inch waist pants was shown "But today" the narrator continued, "He weighs 180 lbs. thanks to what he 'calls the Subway diet.'" Eleven years later, like Cher and Madonna, he is just Jared. The advertising campaign was successful. It exploded profits. And how did they do it? Just as I've been telling you, Subway wrapped the benefits of a sandwich into a human-interest story. Overnight, thanks to the success of this one man's story, they went from a fast-food joint, to a weight-loss company.

In no time flat, overweight folks like Jared were pouring into Subway with the idea of "Eat Subway, lose weight, change your life!" And Jared, a regular guy, not a celebrity, became one of the most recognizable people on the planet. This is the "power of story"—the Jared story—it differentiates Subway, their sandwiches, from all other sandwich and fast food joints in their category. Their sandwiches, the perception is, make fat people, skinny. *Subway wins.*

A classic headline from the satirical newspaper The Onion proclaims, "New Starbucks Opens in Rest Room of Existing Starbucks." These days the same joke could apply to Subway. There are now more than 37,000 franchise locations around the globe. Jared has gotten rich. Subway has sold thousands of franchises. That is the *power* of an effectively told human-interest story.

I became aware, very early in my career, how *many* of the greatest direct-marketing successes were built on the backs of *inspirational* human-interest stories.

Stories, about the product's inventor, about the service-provider. Or about the customers and clients of the product or service the business was selling. One of the most iconic of these stories is the Charles Atlas story, found on the back pages of early comic books. You may remember seeing the below advertisement. The "skinny kid who got sand kicked in his face" at the beach, who was humiliated by

a bully in front of his girlfriend, who then made himself over from weakling to muscle-man. Of course, his marketing message was, "If I was able to do it, then so can you, and I'll show you how," when you purchase my course on weight lifting and building muscle.

Just as easily, this storyline could be applied to a client of a financial planner, who was *once*

embarrassed financially. Then, he hired Joe Smith financial planner where over the next three months, he followed Joe's direction and instruction and, within years, became rich. How can you, or anyone, achieve this similar outcome? Answer: Hire Joe Smith. "If Joe was able to help me [insert a client success story], then certainly he can't help you too."

Got a real estate client? Same thing.

Tell the success story of your client, then invite others to come and experience the same transformational outcome. This is how you defeat Mega-agents. My member, Eric Verdi, every time he sells a home in a neighborhood quickly, or at an above-average-price-point, he sends a marketing piece similar to the one shown here, to all the homeowners in that neighborhood. Under the picture, you'll notice the sub-headline, "How the 'Warren Buffett Approach To Sell Real Estate' helped your neighbor achieve the highest contract-price in your neighborhood." It then goes on to tell a brief human-interest story about Eric's client and their situation, before Eric wraps up and extends an invitation to those homeowners whom might be interested in obtaining a similar result.

Jeremy and Beth, your neighbors, just sold their Myersville home for a record price...

FREE BOOK REVEALS:

How The "Warren Buffett Approach To Sell Real Estate" Helped Your Neighbor Achieve The *Highest* Contract-price In Your Neighborhood...

I think you'll agree, this is an *unusual* story...

This story starts last summer. In July 2013, Jeremy and Beth reached out to me. They wanted to sell their home, but frankly, were hesitant to believe they could get the kind of money they needed from their home, to be able to afford the new they really wanted.

You see a few years ago when the market was 'booming' Jeremy and Beth bought their first home on Mountain Terr, and like everyone else who bought a home during that time, they paid a premium for the privilege to live in that home. But now, over the past few years, prices have fluctuated. So getting top dollar for their home in today's market—a market very different than the market when they purchased it—was an absolute priority.

Like many sellers, they had tough questions about the market. About Appraisals, etc. "How can we get the kind of money we need out of our home?"

This led to an interesting conversation; Jeremy and Beth had contacted me. They had never sold a home. They had only bought a home. And, weren't sure about which approach would net them the most profit for their Myersville home; a value-driven approach or the more common but inferior price-driven approach.

To help Jeremy and Beth in their decision, to weigh the pros and cost of each, I provided them a copy of my book:

The Warren Buffett Approach To Sell Real Estate: How to protect yourself from REAL ESTATE GREED & bank an extra $30k or more by taking a VALUE-DRIVEN approach.

After a few days, they decided the more sophisticated value-driven approach would be best for them. This led to two months of intense preparation. Including scientific staging, a process we call *story*-selling, etc. But, it was worth it. On Tuesday,

February 14th, their Myersville home was officially listed for sale. On Thursday, just two days later, we had a sale. The best part, the winning offer was for the "highest contract price," price per square foot...that any home in their neighborhood had ever sold for.

Jeremy and Beth were ecstatic. Surprised and shocked. They needed a certain price for their home, to be able to net the profit needed, and they got it. But, they didn't think their home would set any kind of a record. This has become somewhat commonplace for my clients. From having studied the world's greatest investor, Warren Buffett, and his investment philosophy. I have discovered by treating your home as an investment, like a business with a "stock price" and by taking a value-driven approach—there is a unique way to extract up to $30,000 or more of additional profit from any home on the market. And, in some cases, as it was for Jeremy and Beth, that extra profit can be the difference between selling and moving up to their next home, or remaining stuck in their current home.

For others, that extra profit it is just their reward for being smart and intelligent and, like Warren Buffett, doing all the things that are necessary to maximize their investment.

If you are thinking of selling your home and may need a certain 'net profit' and in order justify your move and, if you would like me to show you, personally, how this approach that I am known for—The Warren Buffett Approach To Sell Real Estate; a value-driven approach—can put up to $30,000 or more of additional profit in your pocket, don't hesitate to reach out to me. Call 000-000-0000 to schedule an appointment. My assistant's name is Lindsay.

- Eric Verdi

PS: Please plan accordingly. It took Jeremy and Beth two months of intense preparation, working off a detailed checklist I provided. Because of this, plan accordingly. Don't wait. Maximum profit doesn't just happen. It's engineered, from step one.

To get your FREE copy of The Warren Buffett Approach To Sell Real Estate: How to protect yourself against REAL ESTATE GREED & bank an extra $30K by taking a VALUE-DRIVEN APPROACH, just visit our website and leave the necessary information. A copy of the book will be shipped to you, free of charge.

Never forget this: Stories *sell.*

The ability to tell them well, about yourself, about your services, about the results and successes of your clients, etc. is what separates—differentiates—the great marketer and entrepreneur from the mundane and boring, soulless features and benefits, facts and figures, product centered, price justifying, mind-numbing sales pitch of the journeyman.

Look at all your marketing and advertising, what do you see? Are you using human-interest stories to engage prospective clients emotionally? Are your stories connecting and resonating with a target (niche) audience? Are people writing you letters and sending fan mail after they see and read your stories?

When I speak on the *power of story*, I often use the word "resonate." I use it deliberately, just as I do the word, "connection." These two words and *REALLY* understanding them, offer the ultimate path to differentiation.

You will know when you're *effectively* telling the right story, when prospects and clients start telling you *their* version of your story, back to you. As example, how many overweight folks do you think have sought Jared out, and written him letters, just to share with him their struggles about being heavy? *You can bet a lot.* They can relate to him. His story resonates with them and is a source of deep connection.

People are fascinated by stories. Any real estate agent or entrepreneur can immediately boost sales, increase customer loyalty and spark a massive influx of referrals—word of mouth advertising—by crafting and telling compelling stories.

I have often said, "I never sell. I just tell stories." So far, it's worked pretty well for me.

Relevant Podcast Episodes: 1 through ALL

<u>Recommended Resources:</u>

• **Protector Videos Series** (Access inside Member Site)

• **Case Study Interviews** (Access inside Member Site)

• **AMS Podcast** (www.AMSpodcast.com)

• **Value-Driven Approach** (www.TheValueDrivenApproach.com)

• **Forging Elite Storytellers** (www.StoryAthlete.com)

• **90-Day Immersion** (www.90DayImmersion.com)

• **Explore ImpactClub®** (www.ImpactClub.com)

EIGHT

SOURCE OF
DIFFERENTIATION #8
Personality-Driven

By Ryan Fletcher

S top being a professional drone. Stop filtering your every word. Stop trying to please every last soul. Stop being politically correct. I view business a lot like I view life. In life, not everyone can be my friend and in business not everyone can be my client.

A few years ago I attended one of the big '*Get Motivated!*' seminars that traveled across the United States; previously branded *Success Seminars* in the late 90's and early 2000's. The event was held at the Rose Garden in Portland, OR. Colin Powell spoke. Steve Forbes spoke. Bill Cosby and Terry Bradshaw spoke. Brian Tracy spoke on sales, and the one guy, in my opinion, the best speaker, was Krish Dhanam. He said one phrase I'll never forget, I wrote it down:

"Political correctness will be the death of this great nation."

His point: from the days of Ellis Island, America has always been a mixing pot of different cultures, attitudes, values, beliefs, and dozens of different religions and languages. Being "politically correct" is an attempt to eliminate what makes us unique: Our differences. Christmas, Hanukkah, Kwanzaa, each of these gets lumped into "Happy Holidays!" This kind of political corrected-ness is a disintegration of our differences. Reducing meaningful conversation to useless banter. "Fake" relationships. In business, the same thing happens. People lose their identity in favor of a "Mr. or Mrs. Professional," a personality they believe they must take on, to dare not offend a single soul.

One of my good friends has a split personality. His one personality is fun and exciting. Everybody likes to be around him and hear his stories, then, there is his "Mr. Professional" persona. The character that is "on the job" and must, always, try to "please" every prospective client he talks to. Let me tell you, his "professional drone" persona is an utter failure. He's not himself. He's fake. And he comes across as acting and, thus, inauthentic.

This is what politicians do. And it's why nobody trusts them. They're fake!

In the movie *What Happens in Vegas'* starring Ashton Kutcher and Cameron Diaz, Diaz's character Joy McNally plays a high profile stockbroker. She too has a split personality; fun and feisty at home, dull and boring at work. Halfway through the movie, after *finally* letting her boss see her *true* personality, her boss, "Big Dick", says to her, "McNally, had I seen this side of you before, I would've promoted you a long time ago!

Yes, I know this is just a movie. But again, this is instructive. My big breakthrough in business, and it started in real estate—after complete and utter failure—is when I started just *being* me!

The other day, I got an email from an entrepreneur that said, "Dude. Frankly I dig you. I love your foul language. You are real. As soon as I can afford to hire you, I'm in." This is what you want people saying about you, "Dude, I dig you." And don't fool yourself into thinking they're saying this about your "Mr. or Mrs. Professional" persona. They're not.

Comedian Wanda Sykes had a great HBO special titled; *'I'ma Be Me.'* Just do that—be you—and business and profits will boom.

By the way, what is your true personality? Who are you?

There are real estate agents. Then, there are true entrepreneurs who just happen to be in real estate.

If you're a true entrepreneur, not just a real estate agent, I already understand a bit about you. We all tend to be broken toys and outcasts. We think the rules don't apply to us. Etc. But are you hiding it? Or are you embracing that *uniqueness* and weaving it into the fabric of everything you do in your business?

There is a company in Phoenix called Killer Shade. They build "shade" structures, canopies, awnings, and shade sails, presumably, to keep people from bursting into flames in the Arizona sun. I'm serious. They sell "shade." That's their product. Could there be a more boring product than shade? No! There couldn't. But this isn't your typical business. They're smart entrepreneurs. They understand the *real* product—like all businesses—is the *person* and/or *people* behind the product or service that is most important. People do business with people. Killer Shade, their owners and service people, are rich in personality. They sell a commoditized product, anyone can build and sell shade structures, so what is to differentiate them? Answer: Their *likability*. Their individual personalities!

Several years ago I printed off their core values from their website. Other companies might call this a mission statement. But notice the language here. *What We Believe*, more of a religious statement, speaking to *who* they are, oppose to *what* they do. The first value reads:

WHAT WE BELIEVE

> ***Be Real:*** *Ok kids, here is a fan favorite. We Killers have all had jobs where we had to "fake it", act professional, and put on our "game face" every day we trudged into work. Our little Killer Kingdom was founded on being who we are. When we started January of 2005 we decided that we were going to quit trying to be professional, please everyone and use excellent table manners. In our infinite wisdom, we came to the conclusion that by being who we are we would likely alienate 90% of potential customers- but the ones that "got us" would be loyal fans that would allow us to eke out a meager salary while doing what we love. Then the craziest thing happened. People actually liked it. They started coming in droves. Next thing you know- employees loved it, we started attracting the top talent. So what do you end up with- brutally honest people with high integrity that drop the mask. What you see is what you get. We understand we are not a fit for everyone, but we have made our peace, so if you are feelin' our vibe, browse on. If not, best of luck to you...try www.boringshade.com.*

Taking this approach, do you see the power in this?

On another part of the website I saw their lead salesperson, Mike "El Guapo" Boyle, his job title is *Shade Whisper*. Not sales consultant or sales representative or account executive. *Shade Whisperer*. In the careers section of the site, for those looking for a job, they published their Foosball schedule, 9:00 am, 11:45 am and 2:00 pm Monday through Friday. Their party schedule was also published. And they report, "Employee beatings are down a staggering 37% this year." You must understand this is all about having FUN. People more so than anything, want to have fun. They want to be entertained. They want to work with people who make them laugh. With people who provide them an experience. Not with people who *just* sell them products or deliver them services.

Personality-driven marketing differentiates you.

Are you capitalizing on yours? The correct response to someone not liking your *true* personality is not, "Oh my god, I lost a client"—the correct response is—good riddance. Our unique personalities—what makes us, us—is about the only *true* source of differentiation each of us was born with, and yet most real estate agents, businesspeople, and entrepreneurs never put it to work.

It's a shame!

When I work with private clients and members of my Protector/Social Superhero program, one of the first steps is to construct that person's Personal Narrative. To think about this differently, you are the star in your own sitcom. If you character sucks, or is boring, or is uninteresting because no one has taken the time to craft that character—no one will tune into your sitcom to watch your show.

Incidentally, this is why most business owners fail in their attempts to grow their business. They don't understand this concept and or, they tell all the wrong stories.

At the back of this chapter is a condensed version of Cheryl Gordon's Personal Narrative, shrunken down to just 2-pages here. (See Figure 8.1 on page 81). Cheryl is an agent out of Ontario, Canada, who, in just the first couple months of working together, made her local newspaper a half dozen times, was talked about on the radio, and was even interviewed on TV during a popular daytime talk show.

This early success is largely due to the fact, she made it a point to tell her story. She has promoted it, shared it, broadcasted it, and because of it, people have liked who she is. But, this is an important point. I had to push and prod Cheryl for a month, to convince her of the power of having a personal narrative.

When Cheryl first wrote her story and then published it, for family and friends and the entire world to see, in her words, "I felt like I was going to puke."

Sharing the intimate details of your life, yes, can be scary.

But that is what makes you, you. *Own it.* And those who like you, for you, they will be loyal to you for life. And, those who don't, fuck 'em. Good riddance.

Get rid of them!

Ryan Sloper, another member of mine, does a great job of personality-driven marketing as well. He hosts a weekly podcast called "Real Estate 360," which can be found on iTunes. In recent years, his business has blown up to more than 26 million in annual production, largely due to this strategy: Personality-driven marketing. And choosing, deliberately, to market his business like a sitcom, where each new podcast, client newsletter, etc. acts as a new episode of his sitcom to further the storyline of his character.

People love interesting characters!

If you haven't yet started to craft the character that will *star* in your sitcom, start. This is how you defeat Mega-agents and, in the process, become one.

Another member of mine, Eric Verdi, can attest to this. After six straight years of mailing a standard, one-size-fits-all newsletter and being plateaued in his income for those six consecutive years, he decided to make a change. He threw away the old newsletter, crafted his character, defined his moral code and switched to a "sitcom" format.

The end result, Eric went from making 6-figures in a year, to making 6-figures in a quarter.

And he did it inside of 18-months.

Relevant Podcast Episodes: 9, 11, 21, 22, 34, 41, 62-65, 81

<u>Recommended Resources:</u>

• **Protector Videos Series** (Access inside Member Site)

• **Case Study Interviews** (Access inside Member Site)

• **AMS Podcast** (www.AMSpodcast.com)

• **Forging Elite Storytellers** (www.StoryAthlete.com)

• **90-Day Immersion** (www.90DayImmersion.com)

FIGURE 8-1: Personal Narrative of P/SS member Cheryl Gordon.

"I've lived a lot of life in my short 30 years"

Inquiring minds want to know... Really?!

We asked what you wanted... And apparently a large number of you wanted to know more about me?! Ok-You asked for it!

Who is: Cheryl Gordon? MY STORY SO FAR...

I had a short childhood and grew up quickly. I grew up with 2 older brothers and admittedly was a bit of a tomboy (and still am). My Dad was an extremely hard worker so my mother could stay home with us kids.

Most of my childhood memories consist of family camping trips, and me growing up in the gym. I was a gymnast and competed at the provincial level until I was injured at the age of 12 and taken out of the sport by age 13. Kinda funny how short lived a gymnast's career span really is now looking back. Life went on. I graduated high school, took a year off to work and at the age of 17 was a salary supervisor at good ole Value Village (a second hand store).

After working hard for 1 year I went off to college to become a social worker.

Throughout college I was a waitress, bartender, and worked at the college residence. I also worked the midnight shift on the line at GM over the summers to make enough money to put myself through college (p.s. I wouldn't buy a 2004 Detroit if I were you). On top of that I had my fair share of volunteer work which needed to be to be completed for my programs which had me gaining all sorts of experience in the social work field working in group homes, women's shelters and detox centers.

Needless to say after school I was pretty burnt out and I hadn't even had a paying job in my field yet! Right after college I stumbled upon a lucrative modeling career, which landed me a contract with top modeling agency Ford Models. It was a much-needed break from the world of social work!

I was traveling the world and the pay was great and I have some pretty cool pictures to show the kids one day!

After a few years of being a full time model I got back to what I am passionate about. I got to put myself through school for Social work. I worked with youth with mental health and addictions issues and later worked with adults as well. I met a man I would later marry, 2 years later we had our beautiful daughter Ella (who is now 7).

After Ella was born I struggled with sever postpartum depression. That combined with a number of other factors lead to the breakdown of our marriage. After 1 year of marriage counseling and right around Ella's 2nd birthday I found myself applying for divorce, selling our family home, buying my own house, quitting my job and becoming a real estate agent over a 3 month period! It was a world wind. It was one of the worst and best times of my life. I had always wanted to get into real estate but it was never a decision that I felt was supported in my marriage. For those of you that will come to know me you will soon realize no one can tell me that I can't do something.

Naturally I made it my mission to prove those individuals wrong!

Plus I had no other option but to be successful, at this point I had a 2 year old little girl to take care of and a mortgage payment to make! My first year in real estate was hard! Really hard! There were a number of times I wish I could have just quit but quitting for me wasn't an option.... Must be the "Gumburger" in me that's my mindset on name). I told myself I was going to be different than "all these other agents" out there. I was going to build a business based on respect and integrity and if it meant it would take longer for me to build that business then so be it....

At the end of the day I knew I would have a better and stronger business because of it! My first year I did 12 deals, my second year I doubled my first years income and found myself getting started for the second time so now husband Brad! My 3rd year we did it somehow gave back to the schools in our community through real estate. After a few months of thought...

My 4th year I was in the top 20% of the company and asked to sit on our companies Agent Leadership Council and head up the Culture Committee.

After having Mason I found myself a little bit disconnected from the office and took the opportunity to sit on the council and committee. Through the work with my office and getting back in momentum with my business I found myself wanting more... I no longer wanted to just DO the business but rather craved BUILDING my businesses.

I wanted to be more than just a real estate agent, I wanted to be someone who gives back and to build a legacy, something my children and husband could be proud of.

Through one of our community community events, RED Day which has our office giving a day of service to our community organized myself and the culture committee we donated a day of service to one of the schools in an underprivileged area of our community. While organizing this day it became obvious to me just how much teachers do for our children and our community and just how underfunded some of our schools are especially those that do not have parents who can contribute towards the extras all of the schools rely so heavily on. At that time I thought wouldn't it be great if I somehow gave back to the schools in our community through real estate. After a few months of thought...

The Teacher Only Program® was born.

I decided early on this had to be different though. It couldn't just be a real estate program. We quickly started innovating and within the year, we had developed a proprietary approach called the "Warren Buffett Approach" to sell real estate. This approach—by studying the world's greatest investor, Warren Buffett, and applying his investment philosophy to real estate—we discovered there is a unique way to extract up to $30,000 or more of additional profit, from any ordinary home on the market. So far, this approach has been a huge success for our clients...

Our last client banked $22,500 of extra profit in just 7days.

But again, this had to be different. It had to be more than just a real estate program for teachers. How could we give back? How could we make a difference? How could we make an impact in the community?—in the lives of teachers and students? This question is seemed like it haunted me for weeks. Then it happened. I read an article where 9 out every 10 kids in Durham School District received some kind of meal assistance. Hungry students, in turns out, is a very big issue in our community. As a parent, I can't imagine that feeling. As a student, sure, meals are provided to you at school through these programs, but what about when you go home? How could you possibly focus on school, or make school a priority, when you go to bed hungry each night?

The next day I arranged a meeting with the local food bank, St. Paul's on-the-Hill. I talked to the director, Margaret Jost. I learned a lot, Margaret confirmed just how big of an issue this really was. That's all it took, the next week my mind was made up...

Outdoor Movie Night For Hunger™ was born.

I never imagined the Event would be so successful so quickly, supported by so many amazing people in our community. Over 1500 people attended. Over 3,000 lbs. of food was collected for St. Paul's on the Hill Community Food Bank this past year alone. The event was sponsored by over 30 incredible businesses, including Mercedes-Benz Lowes, amd Sun-Life Financial. Outdoor Movie Night for Hunger, was written up in the Durham paper four times, once making the front page. It was also broadcasted about, and publicized on local radio stations KX96, 9.49 and CKDO, not to mention, garnished the support of more than 20 Community Partners, including, The Durham District School Board, Blair Ridge Public School and The Brooklin Public Library to name a few.

With the support of my community behind me we were able to make a huge impact in the lives of so many.

Together We Can Make an Even Bigger Difference!

With more thought given to this it has become our mission, with the Teacher Only Program® and Outdoor Movie Night for Hunger™ as the foundation—to donate $10,000 each year to local and teacher-related charities. Alongside banking my business and helping clients achieve their real estate dreams; Real Estate has afforded me the opportunity to give back in a way I never thought possible. It has provided me with the resources to create a movement and an opportunity to work with likeminded individuals who are just as passionate about giving back to their community as I am.

In the months to come I will share with you more about my story, what lead me to where I am today and some of my discoveries along the way. I would also like to welcome you walk along side me as my saga continues! I am excited and looking forward to what lies ahead.

To connect with me directly regarding Outdoor Movie Night for Hunger, the Teacher Only Program® or other matters, media-ting real estate, philanthropy, fund-raising or community leadership, email is preferred, and yes, I answers every email personally in 24-48 hours or as soon as I can. at CherylorGordon.ca

Outdoor Movie Night for Hunger! Stny Newspaper 2012

NINE

SOURCE OF
DIFFERENTIATION #9
Celebrity Status

By Ryan Fletcher

We live in a celebrity-obsessed world. Oprah. Brad Pitt. Tom Cruise. When most people think of celebrities they think of famous athletes and other publicly known entertainers. Some even think of Snooki and J-Wow of reality-TV fame, *The Jersey Shore*, who reportedly command as much as $30,000 for a one night, three-hour club appearance as celebrities.

But for a moment, forget what most people think about celebrities. How they view them. What their definition is. Etc. For our purpose, as a pathway to differentiation, the *Merriam-Webster* definition is instructive: Celebrity, *noun*: 1) a person who is widely known and usually much talked about, 2) the fact or state of being known by the public.

Fact is, achieving this definition of celebrity on a small scale, local scale, is a pretty easy thing to accomplish.

When you implement the strategies discussed in the previous eight chapters of this book: Exclusive niche marketing, Affinity connection, Names, Proprietary secret, Added-value to transcend from "services" and "products," to providing "experiences," and have an authentic Charitable mission—each, embodied, conveyed, in the form of a powerful *Story*—the result is, you become *known* for something, by a specific someone, within your target audience.

The outcome achieved: Celebrity status.

It is very important to understand, there is no such thing as a commoditized business, product or service, or service provider. There are only those who act as commodities (and allow themselves to be labeled as commodities) due to poor positioning and marketing. If you are viewed as a commodity in your business, meaning, clients are not seeking you out and completing applications to work with you, you are doing something wrong when it comes to how you're positioning yourself in the marketplace.

The vast majority of real estate agents that I've ever known, including most business owners, and entrepreneurs, live their whole lives inside of a tiny little box of possibilities. Nobody put them inside that little box, except themselves, the result of their limited thinking. I find most business owners and entrepreneurs have a desire for respect and power. They want a strong and robust business. They want to be worry-free about income. They have pride and integrity, and wish they didn't have to beg family and friends for referrals.

They even give lip service to the ideas of work ethic, and willingness to do "whatever it takes," to achieve those things, for themselves, their business, and for their families.

However, when it comes time to take action, they're all talk.

Author, Napoleon Hill, wrote the landmark bestseller *Think and Grow Rich*. I think most entrepreneurs, or, as billionaire Mark Cuban calls them, "Wantrepreneurs," take this title too literal. They actually believe that if they "think" about growing rich, that it will happen. In other words, most are all "talk," and no "walk."

Their intentions are to take action. They want to take action. They know they need to take action. But two, three, five years from now, most, will still be planning and getting their ducks all in a row.

I caution against that path of *perpetual* planning.

You can only be seen and treated as a celebrity, sought-out and paid like a celebrity, if you commit, for lack of a better phrase, to continually *fascinate and captivate* your audience. This is what celebrities do. They captivate and fascinate us. And no, one doesn't need to be a famous athlete or movie star to do this.

Steve Jobs captivated and fascinated us with his vision, with his ideas.

In my business, I directly influence more than 15,000 entrepreneurs each week. At the time of this writing, this past week, I traveled to the tiny town of Roseburg, OR. There, I met with a group of business friends and fellow entrepreneurs. The moment I arrived, my friend blasted out an invitation to all of his clients to come meet the "marketing celebrity" that just arrived in town, to stop by his office, to pick the brain of "the guy" who wrote an ad that generated over 15 Million in sales, for an organization, to many, considered the Rolls Royce of the direct-marketing industry. To this particular audience, entrepreneurs, business owners—all interested and fascinated with direct-response marketing, all interested and fascinated with growing their businesses, all interested and fascinated with copywriting, and how one generates that kind of revenue from a single ad—I was seen as a celebrity, and treated as such.

Sounds weird, but I couldn't care less to meet the President of the United States. I would much prefer to spend a day with Dan Kennedy. Or the half-dozen other marketing legends, for which I am captivated and fascinated by, because of how they've marketed and positioned themselves, relevant to my specific interests.

Keyword: Audience.

To engineer celebrity status for yourself and business, you have to know, *by whom*, you want to be seen as a celebrity. For me, I want to be known and talked about in direct-response marketing circles and amongst serious entrepreneurs. For the record, most real estate agents, in my opinion, do not fall into either of those two categories. This is why I don't cater to most agents. I cater only to the few. But that is the secret, knowing, to which audience you want to be famous.

If you operated a weight-loss clinic, for example, then why not set out to be the Jillian Michaels of your local community.

In that case, *WHO* is your audience? How can those people that you have identified as your niche be reached? What is the [marketing] message that deeply connects and resonates with them? What human-interest stories can you tell, as a case study, about your own transformation, or about the transformation of your clients, that demonstrates the effectiveness of your system and your ability to get results?

Further, how are you able to do this? What is the proprietary *secret* behind your method? Where did you learn this secret? Why does no one else know it, or utilize it, as you do? How successful have you been, compared to competitors, by using this method?

If you've been in real estate for any length of time, I assume you have many great testimonials that could be used as case studies.

And before you know it, whether you're a personal trainer, a financial planner, a business consultant, like me, or a real estate agent, people are talking about you.

By definition, you are now a Celebrity.

The key element of being seen as a celebrity, is being *known* and recognized and, of course, talked about.

This is what famous promoter P.T. Barnum knew to be true, and capitalized on. People had to see what all the "fuss" was about, for themselves. If you think about the story of P.T. Barnum, it's really pretty amazing. He started as a clerk at a fruit stand. Then he met Joice Heth, who claimed to be the 161-year-old nurse to George Washington. What does a 161-year old person look like? I don't know. But that's what Barnum counted on, people's curiosity.

"Come see the amazing 161-year old nurse to George Washington. You will be astounded! You will be amazed!"

The next thing you know, people were talking about Joice Heth and P.T. Barnum. People had to see for themselves what all the "fuss" was about. Fast forward 150 years. Today, still, P.T. Barnum is one of the best-known, most iconic figures of all time.

The question is, though, what are you doing in your business that is worthy of being talked about?

Most business owners and entrepreneurs I come in contact with, play small ball. They never ask that question. They never challenge themselves to think bigger, or bolder, or more daring. Most people, when presented with the idea of being seen as a "celebrity in their marketplace," respond timidly.

"Why would anyone see me as a celebrity?" they ask, "I'm not a celebrity."

Really?

Where's the self-confidence?

Where the self-assurance in your skills and abilities?

But this just speaks to the bigger point; about what people believe is possible.

Henry Ford was spot-on when he said, "Whether you think you can, or you think you can't—you're right." Celebrity status is the ultimate path to defeat Mega-agents, but you must believe it's possible to achieve it.

Or… it won't be.

Relevant Podcast Episodes: 28, 41, 42, 48, 71, 83

<u>Recommended Resources:</u>

• **Protector Videos Series** (Access inside Member Site)

• **Case Study Interviews** (Access inside Member Site)

• **AMS Podcast** (www.AMSpodcast.com)

• **Value-Driven Approach** (www.TheValueDrivenApproach.com)

- **Forging Elite Storytellers** (www.StoryAthlete.com)

- **90-Day Immersion** (www.90DayImmersion.com)

- **Explore ImpactClub®** (www.ImpactClub.com)

.

SOURCE OF
DIFFERENTIATION #10
Preference / Social Proof

By Ryan Fletcher

People don't buy what's best for them. They don't even know what's best for them. They usually only know what they want, based, largely, on what they *think* other people want.

According to Robert Cialidini, author of the book *Influence: The Psychology of Persuasion*, we determine what is correct by finding out what other people think is correct. Incidentally, this is why online "reviews" have exploded in recent years. *Amazon* has book reviews. Travel sites like *Expedia* have hotel and resort reviews. For whatever company you search for on Google, Google now has reviews for those places of business. *Yelp!* is an entire site dedicated to finding nothing but the "best" local companies, from restaurants to nightlife, to health and medical services, etc., based on the input, experiences and reviews of others.

Armed with this information, or I should say, "the opinions of others", people then make their decision about what is "best" for them.

An undeniable truth: Humans _are_ lemmings.

We've been hardwired to follow the herd. This presents an opportunity for you and I, as people who understand marketing. When you supply, "What other people _think_ is correct" in your marketing, about your product or service, you're able to engage the power of this influential trigger: Social proof. And, thus, create preference. This is what influence is all about. Creating _preference_ for your business, products and services.

And preference can be manufactured.

As an aside, if you're not studying the marketing and advertising of non-profit organizations—you should be. Charitable organizations hire some of the best direct-response marketers and copywriters in the world. Behind credit card companies, charitable organizations, from all walks, benefiting different causes, are some of the biggest users of direct mail—spending hundreds of millions annually.

Since I donate to Smile Train® each year, I receive a ton of donation requests. In a recent fundraising letter, the first thing presented to me when I opened the envelope were pictures of ten easily recognized celebrities: Robin Williams, Hilary Swank, Walter Cronkite, Colin Powell, Howie Mandel, among others. The headline above the photos of these celebrities read: "Celebrity Supporters: They Can Choose Any Charity In The World To Support. Here's Why They Choose The Smile Train®."

This is about "supplying" preference. This is about creating *the perception* that Smile Train® is the best charitable organization to donate to—because *these* celebrities are doing it.

Of course, does that make it true? *No!*

Does it mean that Smile Train® donates more money, for every dollar donated, directly to the cause? *No!* Does it mean that this charity helps more children, or gets better results for the children that they do help, than any other charity? *No!*

But we're not dealing with reality here. We're dealing with perception.

Reality has little to do with influence.

Whether your product or service is truly the best, or gets the best results for prospects and clients, doesn't really matter.

Going back to the concept of *Exclusive Niche Marketing* (Differentiation Strategy No.1). Let's say I was a real estate agent again, and let's say I created a Nurse Only Program® as a vehicle to position my real estate services. Now, just like the Smile Train® and their celebrity endorsers, I could pull the *Affinity* card (Differentiation Strategy No. 2), and have ten or twelve nurses endorse my Nurse Only Program®. The headline could read, *"These Nurses Could Have Chosen Any Agent In Vancouver to Sell Their Home. Here's Why They Chose Ryan Fletcher's Nurse Only Program®."* Then, next to their pictures, I could include their testimonial i.e. a *review* of their experience from having worked with me.

This makes you the "preferred" service-provider to that niche.

Eric Verdi, a member of my Protector/Social Superhero program, and someone I've talked about in a previous chapter, took a different approach to this same concept.

For every home sold through his Teacher Only Program®, he donated $250.00 to a local school or charity of the client's choice. After having a large check created, Eric would then contact the principal of the school to arrange a photo opportunity as he handed over the check. This photo, along with a story about his client and his charitable mission, were then published in his Teacher Only Program® newsletter and distributed to every teacher throughout the district. Again, this is about *supplying* preference. Just by standing next to the principal of the school, through implied endorsement, Eric becomes more trusted and preferred by the teachers on that community.

Eric is not alone in using this approach to earn trust and preference. Below is a HipChat conversation (our private member-community platform) between two P/SS members, Cheryl Gordon and Tricia Yocum pertaining to this same concept. Over time we have become much more sophisticated in making this strategy work for us. (See Figures 10.1 and 10.2 and 10.3) It now starts with a 2-page letter that Cheryl and I crafted—and then shared with the group—to contact the principal at the different schools, for cooperation and a photo opportunity. There is then a Press Release as well as reporting in our own internal publications and media platforms.

	Tuesday May 27, 2014	
Cheryl Gordon	20140527_163341.jpg 1.8MB	May-27 1:35 PM

Cheryl Gordon   @all just picked this up for my donations to schools.   May-27 1:35 PM

Ron Rank   @CherylGordon Do you use an erasable marker with this? It looks great!   May-27 3:27 PM

Tricia Yocum   @CherylGordon great, I have one very similar and I take a picture with my buyers at   May-27 3:30 PM
the house with the Sold sign and then the giant check I am going to donate to the school of their
choice...I write about how "John and Beth" just moved into their new home and we are donating $XXX
to Whatever Elementary School in their name...great publicity. I post the pictures on FB too!

Cheryl Gordon   @RonRank yuppers dry erase   May-27 4:17 PM

Cheryl Gordon   @TriciaYocum That's similar to what I am doing. I am also sending a letter to the   May-27 4:19 PM
schools requesting a time to present them with the cheque, taking a pic, interviewing the school then
submitting a press release to all of the local media as a call to action for others to donate to local
schools. I donate 250 to the school of my clients choice. Then that press release will go on my website,
the story will be told in my newsletter, on Facebook, and on my website with a running tally of the
amount that has been donated.

Now, one thing, before we move on. I want to clarify something. I'm all for *truly* being the best at what you do. I have worked hard to master every skill I've ever needed, in order to get my client the best result. But when it comes to influence, all I'm saying is, we're not dealing with reality. We're dealing with perception.

Two different things!

The strategy of supplying preference is more about declaring yourself the leader, someone to be paid attention to, than anything else. You could starve waiting for *actual* preference. It won't happen. You must decide it's something you want. Then, you can take the necessary steps to engineer it.

Keep in mind, supplying preference goes way beyond, just supplying preference for your core set of services i.e. real estate services. With rare exception, the most important *product* of every real estate agent, business owner and entrepreneur, is the relationship between you and the consumer. And, to begin a relationship with a prospect or client, it helps and makes it much easier if they actually like you. And no, we don't want to leave that to chance either. We want to engineer it.

One of the ways to do that is through the use of your Charitable Mission (Differentiation Strategy No. 6), and to make sure you enunciate that mission, clearly, to all prospective clients. Their immediate thought and judgment about you will be, "*Wow! What an incredible person.*"

To be the *preferred* person, you must do *likeable* things.

Are you a real estate agent? Or are you a philanthropist?

A terrific way to *supply* preference for you, as a person, is to position yourself as a philanthropist. Society tends to demonize business owners and sales professionals in the private sector, assigning them the labels of "greed" and "profit-driven." But the philanthropist... philanthropists, universally, are loved and adored.

With this in mind, let's revisit the Nurse Only Program® example. Imagine a photo of me standing next to 20 or 30 nurses, where as a group, we're holding one of those large oversized checks, donating it to the director of a local charity. Now, with that image in your mind, imagine, next to that photo, this headline: "*Local Real Estate Agent and Team of 27 Vancouver Nurses Raise $3,283 in Effort to Give Children Born With Cleft Palates Back Their Smiles.*" Fletcher, team leader, says "*This donation to the Smile Train® will cover the entire cost of 13 life-changing surgeries and forever change 13 lives.*"

Then to crank it up a notch, what if I applied Differentiation Strategy No. 7—putting the "power of story" to these headlines and submitted it as a press release? Is there any doubt in your mind that we couldn't make the local newspaper or nightly news? Hint: Many of my members have.

And Yes. *Publicity* **supplies even more "preference".**

Publicity is also a key driver of Differentiation Strategy #9, celebrity status, too.

Preference and social proof—this strategy—is a powerful influential trigger in and of itself. But hopefully, you see how multiple *Differentiation Strategies*, when stacked together, one on the back of the other, are strengthened and able to feed on each other.

This is what you want in business. *Momentum*. It's the snowball effect. It's the way you defeat Mega-agents, plus how you differentiate from all other competitors.

Relevant Podcast Episodes: 8, 15, 69, 70,

Recommended Resources:

• **Protector Videos Series** (Access inside Member Site)

• **Case Study Interviews** (Access inside Member Site)

• **AMS Podcast** (www.AMSpodcast.com)

• **Forging Elite Storytellers** (www.StoryAthlete.com)

• **90-Day Immersion** (www.90DayImmersion.com)

• **Explore ImpactClub®** (www.ImpactClub.com)

FIGURE 10-1: Letter sent to school Principals to secure photo opportunity for the donation, interview opportunity, and media cooperation for the Press Release, to obtain publicity.

CHERYL *Gordon*

DOING GOOD THINGS

Re: **Congratulations! Your school has been selected as a recipient of a $250 donation!**

Dear Mr. Greg Island,

Your school was recently nominated by Sarah and Graham Passmore whose daughter, Danika Passmore, is a 2ⁿᵈ grader at Blair Ridge. Read on to learn more! ☺

Maybe you have heard of me?... My name is Cheryl Gordon. I am a local Real Estate Agent but more importantly, the Founder and CEO of the Durham Teacher Only Program®, Founder and Host of Outdoor Movie Night for Hunger™, which collected over 3,000 lbs. of food for our local food banks last year, Chair of the 2013 Culture Committee that raised $39,852 and donated 1,500 turkey dinners (to feed an estimated 6,000 people) this past Christmas. I have also, in the last year, spearheaded other initiatives that continue to fuel a passion of mine—giving back and impacting our community!

Finding New Ways "To Give" Is Truly a Passion of Mine!

About a year ago I experienced first hand 'the underfunding' in our local schools, and the significant impact it can have on students and their families. Perhaps when we get together, I can share this story with you. But the short of it is, it has inspired me to do more. I believe I can. I believe we all can. In my experience, when a community comes together and *truly* is on a mission to accomplish something great, nothing can stop it...

When we set out to collect 3,000 lbs. of food for the local food bank, many thought we were crazy, but we achieved it. When we set out to feed 1,500 families (an estimated 6,000 people) this past Christmas, again, many thought we were crazy, but again we achieved it. *We proved them wrong.* And I say "we" because I could not have achieved these things alone. But through the power of the community and a few strategic partners, magic is possible and it *can* happen.

I've seen it...

My latest goal and mission is (over the next 12 months) to personally donate $10,000 to local charities and schools in our community. Through our Durham Teacher Only Program® program, I will be donating $250.00 from each home sold to the school of my clients choice. I mentioned a second ago, my clients Graham and Sarah Passmore have recently sold their home and nominated Blair Ridge as the recipient of their $250.00 donation.

But it doesn't end there. I want to inspire others to give too.

I am just one local business owner. I can only donate so much. I wish I had the resources to donate ten times as much, $100,000 each year, but I'm afraid I don't yet have that ability. Maybe one day. Then it hit me. Every time I've ever *publicly* talked about "giving back and making a difference," and people have seen me start or recruit volunteers, or sponsors, for an initiative of mine—without fail, I've received written stories from people who have been *inspired* to do more themselves.

One such person is a friend of mine, Kara Onofrio, founder of Autism's Angels, who recently handed over a check for $18,954.11 to Autism Ontario, thanks to a philanthropy event she organized. Having seen her results, I couldn't help but wonder....

FIGURE 10-1: Page 2.

What if more people could be inspired, people like Kara, like me, like you? What impact would it have? How many students and families might it help in a profound & memorable way?

This is the question I asked, before I decided to send you this letter, "How could we do that?" I decided I would need to do a better job of making the *need* known that funds are *needed* for our local charities and for our schools. And, of course, how those "donated funds" could impact the lives of those families and students in need.

Further, I figured it would go a long way to inspire others if, I talked about giving, publicly, and, did my best to lead by example. Each month I publish a Newsletter that reaches nearly 1,000 Durham families, business owners and philanthropists, who, I believe, could be *inspired* to do more.

This is where you come in. I *need* your help!

With your help and, of course, your permission, I would like to sit down and interview you, briefly, for just a few minutes, about where the greatest need is for donated funds in our schools. Who are the students it helps, who are the families that benefit—and how?

Also, when we meet and I interview you—I would ask for your permission to snap a photo of you being presented the $250.00 donation, courtesy of Danika's parents, Sarah and Graham Passmore, and to use that photo in two ways to further raise awareness for our local schools.

1. To print the picture in my monthly Newsletter (distributed to nearly 1,000 people of influence and potential donors) and use the photo plus the story of Blair Ridge being the recipient of the donation on my website, and in other social media.

2. Your permission to submit the photo and story of Blair Ridge being the recipient of the donation in a press release to my contacts within the media; such as local newspapers, TV, and radio shows to hopefully reach *and inspire* more people "to donate" to our local schools.

If I'm not out there working to raise awareness, then how can I badger others to be?

This is why I need your help.

I know all too well that most people tend to give *only* when "a true need" has been expressed upon them. People are standing by. They want to give. They want to donate. But they don't know how. And further, they want to *know* their gift will have impact. What better way to inspire these people, than to write a story about that need and to get it out into the local media?

Daily, we are inundated with negative news media. But here, we have an opportunity to change that. You are needed. I am needed. And together, just maybe we can inspire a community—to give more, to fund raise more, and to build on the momentum that we've created...

To start the momentum...

Please contact me directly. My personal number is 905-391-7955 or via email: Cheryl@CherylGordon.ca to schedule a time that I may come to present you with the donation to your school, and spend a few minutes to discuss the topic of giving and where the greatest *needs* exist.

Thank you so much for your help,

-Signature

PS: I intended to just write you a short note. But I feared "short and brief" would not have accurately reflected my passion or mission here. *Thank you for reading.*

FIGURE 10-2: Photo taken by the elementary school for the newspaper, internal publications, and was tweeted to the school's Twitter followers before Cheryl even posted it to Facebook, sent a press release, or even talked about in her own newsletter.

FIGURE 10-3: Reprinted from Cheryl's Client Newsletter

Another home sold by Cheryl means another donation made to local schools in our community!

Spotted: Cheryl Gordon Doing Good Things!
And why she says her clients are really the ones to thank...

Oshawa, ON June 26th, 2014.
By Cheryl Gordon

I recently had the honour of meeting Denis Nickerson (Principal), Lorelei Downes (Vice Principal), Mrs.Odynski (Kindergarten Teacher), as well as these excited and helpful students, Lexi & Logan (brother & sister), McKenzie, Halle, Michael, Matthew, Alexis while making a donation to their school- Glen Street Public School in Oshawa. (Photo Above)

As a part of my ongoing mission to give back to our local community, through my Durham Teacher Only Program, and with the help of my wonderful clients it has become my mission to donate/raise $10,000 a year for local schools and charities across the Durham Region. With every home I sell a donation is made to a local elementary school of my Seller choice. For recent clients Jordan and Dan Martin it was a quick decision to choose Glen Street as Jordan was a Kindergarten Teacher at this school and knows first had the need that exists not only in the school but this community.

It became clear to me through other charity work I have done in the past that all of our local schools are underfunded. Most schools rely heavily upon us parents to be able to subsidies the needs of the school and often times it still isn't enough. Breakfast programs in some schools are not able to meet the demand and children in our own communities are coming to school hungry and also coming to school without lunches. Critical special education teachers for our children are not being provid-

ed due lack of funding. Some of our school library's are scarcely low on new and engaging books for our children and some of the gym equipment and toys are either non existent or old enough to have been used when my parents parents parents went to school...

These are just some of the reasons I have made it my mission to donate to our local schools. But, I am just one business owner and while I would like to be able to donate more I can't. Maybe some day I will be able to do more. But what I do know is that bringing awareness to some of these issues is just half the battle. So with that- If you are in a position or are able to donate or volunteer please consider our local schools!

Glen Street P.S plans to use the money to enhance their outdoor play yard with equipment to help improve gross motor skills. They chose to use the money for the Kindergarten program since the money was donated on the recommendation of Jordan Martin who worked as a kindergarten teacher at the school and her husband Dan.

If it wasn't for the trust and loyalty of my clients and the referrals of friends, family, and past clients this initiative wouldn't be possible! So a big thank you to my clients for their continues trust and loyalty! This program and my mission raise/donate $10,000 a year is something that has been made possible because of each and everyone of YOU!

For more information about this initiative or how you or someone you know can get their home sold quickly for top dollar just like Jordan and Dan who where able to pocket _$41,100 over their asking price_ using my proprietary Warren Buffett Approach and have helped to give back to our local community at the same time please contact me at: Cheryl@CherylGordon.ca or 905-391-7955. Together we can help you achieve your real estate dreams and make a difference in the lives of so many in our community!

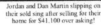

Jordan and Dan Martin slipping on their sold sing after selling for their home for $41,100 over asking!

ELEVEN

SOURCE OF
DIFFERENTIATION #11
Size Matters

By Ryan Fletcher

Yes, size matters! But it's also true. The "Motion of the Ocean" can make impact as well.

You might argue this is a debate better suited for the cover of *Cosmopolitan*; debated by gossip columnists. "Does Size REALLY Matter? 10 Surefire Ways to Make Up For Lack of Size!!!"

Truth is, here's my advice, if you have "size," use it to your advantage. If you don't, then stop dwelling on it.

If your business is small, with only a few clients and you're unable to afford $1,000's each month in advertising to compete head-on, for visibility and attention, against larger competitors—then just accept that. Embrace that. Harness the "Motion of the ocean" argument, and make what you *have* work the best it can.

A big reason why so many folks fail in business, in life, hell, even in the bedroom is because they focus *only* on what they DO NOT have, and or, CANNOT offer.

Understand. The "male enhancement" industry is a billion-dollar per year industry solely because people are focused on what they "DO NOT have, and CAN NOT offer." And instead of focusing on what they *do* have, and *can* offer—the often more important traits that they bring to the table—they endlessly waste time, effort, energy and money on trying to "grow" a bigger… by buying products like Extenze, Enzyte, Longinexx… and by taking various pills, powders, potions, while trying to learn the secret exercises of… all just so they can satisfy their own ego and mask their own insecurities.

This is exactly how 99% of real estate agents and business owners execute their marketing and advertising: Ego-driven, ego-focused. This is also why short men with "little man" syndrome tend to drive big trucks. They're *all* just trying to make up for something they lack—just trying to be, and appear, bigger than their competitors.

Size alone, is a poor way to go about getting clients.

If you ever visit Rodeo Drive in Beverly Hills, you will find many "small" boutique shops, doing exceptionally well. Wal-Mart is a big store. But the niche Wal-Mart caters to vs. the niche that the boutiques on Rodeo Drive cater to is entirely different.

When I was in New York a few years ago, I noticed the store: *Bargains for Millionaires.* This store was quite small compared to Macy's, the department store, which covered three city blocks. And yet, this little store with only 1,200 to 1,500 square feet was thriving. People were over-flowing out of the doors, and into the streets, and I'm sure, buying very expensive shoes and handbags.

This is instructive because in business, and in social circles, the word "small" is often synonymous with a *more* personal, greater attention to detail, higher quality experience. Need proof or want proof? When you think of Wal-Mart, none of that comes to mind. Big businesses are seen as corporate swine farms, run by faceless cold-hearted number crunchers, more likely to treat customers and clients like cattle rather than people.

Of course, this is not necessarily true, but that is the perception, so marketers like you and I can harness it to our advantage.

I have a friend, who, just recently, paid $25,000 to join a high-level mastermind group. This group was pitched as a "small" group, set to meet just three times per year and, to qualify, you needed to be doing a million dollars or more in revenue.

Being small, when positioned correctly, can work to your advantage.

When I first started in real estate, for example, I had no experience. I had no clients. I had no results. I had no testimonials. I had no credibility. I didn't have any expertise either, or unique knowledge. I didn't even know how to fill out a listing agreement.

Literally, I had nothing going for me. *Nothing!*

So, rather than dwell on those shortcomings, I sought to capitalize on that reality. When given lemons, you make lemonade. I was a blank canvas and was free to create whatever *perception* about my services, and myself, as I wished.

So I wrote this:

A little confession in advance: I do not sell 100 or 200 homes a year like some real estate agents do. It simply is not a goal of mine. I have no interest in operating a "swine farm" where clients are herded like cattle. I am much more interested in results. Attention to detail. Client experience. And maximizing profit, in strict accord to my client's goals. I am a control freak also. I demand excellence, which means, to operate my business as I envision, I do not have 15 team members "to do" all the work for me. When you're accepted as a client of mine, should we "click," you get me and only me. THAT MEANS I WILL ACTUALLY CALL YOU BACK. Unlike most agents, I prefer to see my real estate business as a small "boutique shop" for an elite few (not the masses). But honestly, we're getting ahead of ourselves, aren't we? Read the enclosed report and, if you like what you read, we can *explore* the possibility of working together. Until that first step is taken and completed though, then really, you can't make an informed decision to retain my services, and I can't make an informed decision to accept you as a client – so, first step first.

Now, to clarify: That paragraph above is *just* one snippet from a much more robust report and free information package that I would send to clients via direct mail.

It demonstrates the point though: You can fret and worry about your "lack of size" and be hamstrung by it, or you can accept it, harness it, and use it to your distinct advantage.

And since the competition only ever focuses on what they *don't* have and *can't* offer—their insecurities—this shift in thinking gives you a sizable advantage.

Any real estate agent and serious entrepreneur can gain power, by simply understanding how this *positioning*-concept works.

In business, size really doesn't matter—you can win either way! Big or small, properly positioned, differentiates you and elevates you above your competitors.

Mega-agents or not, you can defeat them.

Relevant Podcast Episodes: 4, 5, 94

<u>Recommended Resources:</u>

• **Protector Videos Series** (Access inside Member Site)

• **Case Study Interviews** (Access inside Member Site)

• **AMS Podcast** (www.AMSpodcast.com)

• **Value-Driven Approach** (www.TheValueDrivenApproach.com)

• **Forging Elite Storytellers** (www.StoryAthlete.com)

• **90-Day Immersion** (www.90DayImmersion.com)

• **Explore ImpactClub®** (www.ImpactClub.com)

TWELVE

SOURCE OF
DIFFERENTIATION #12
Price Strategy

By Ryan Fletcher

I t takes "balls" to hang your shingle out as *The Most Expensive* real estate agent in your marketplace. But if you have such courage, price alone can differentiate you.

When I first started as a copywriter and direct-response consultant, I was lucky enough to find a quote about *price* strategy, from legendary adman, David Ogilvy. Ogilvy said, paraphrased, "Any damn fool can cut their price and put on a deal, but it takes genius, faith and perseverance to build a brand." Ogilvy was the marketing mind behind companies like Rolls Royce. Which he stated, "There's a reason a Rolls Royce never goes on sale. It's worth it."

What he meant was, I refuse to cheapen the brand just to sell a few cars. Besides. "The price is what it is," meaning, you get what you pay for.

Back in early 2008, I was doing some work for a division of Agora, Inc., a $500 million per year company, and the world's largest publisher of financial newsletters. This was the beginning of the financial collapse. The trend was: "Oh shit, nobody has any money. People are scared.   No one will spend $2,000 for a stock trading service." As a result, everyone, including my client got on the bandwagon of price-cutting and was quick to put their services "on sale." I chose to go in the opposite direction.

I came back with this headline: "…an Unthinkable Amount."

Why 487 *"BETA-Testers"*...
Paid an Unthinkable
Amount for Jack Crooks'
Knowledge...

Renegade Currency Trader Discovers Wealth In **Shockingly** Small **"Sub-Niche"** that produces profits upwards of **$953 per minute!**

Friday, 9:13am

Dear Friend,

This is a rather unusual story.

The letter went on to tell the incredible story, about the discovery that Jack and his son had made. And how, in just 12-months, they were able to bring their small test-group of subscribers i.e. beta-testers a great number of winning trades. The service was $2,500 a year, no discount, and readers were told that there never would be a discount.

Further, readers who received the invitation to join [the next small group] were told, "Only 1 out of every 100 invited to join" would be accepted. Creating exclusivity.

Long story short, the previous best sales letter for Jack's service, sold approx. $1 million in new subscriptions. Mine surpassed that previous best in the first week, and went on to sell over $15 million in the next 6 months. And yes, I got a nice royalty on all of that, and Jack, well, I believe he added a new wing onto his home, overlooking a lake in an upscale community.

Most important, beyond just the immediate financial gain, this promotion built Jack's reputation as a "Someone."

To understand how this is possible, and to understand how ANY business owner, sales professional or entrepreneur—not just a real estate agent—can duplicate this kind of positioning for themselves, we can breakdown that headline into its components.

Seven different differentiation strategies:

1) Preference & Social Proof: "487 Beta-Testers Paid"...i.e. others are doing it, and benefitting, thus, so could you...

2) Price Strategy: "Paid an Unthinkable Amount for Jack Crooks' Advice." People have been brainwashed to believe "you get what you pay for"—the assumption is, "Damn, if all these people are paying an "unthinkable amount," for Jack's advice, then Jack must be pretty damn good at what he does...

3, 4) Exclusive Niche / Affinity: Jack Crooks is a "currency trader" who only targets other currency traders; inviting them be "belong" to a small group of beta-testers where, he is seen as "one of them" and, speaks their language...

5) Proprietary Secret: "Discovers Wealth in Shockingly Small Sub-Niche, produces profits upwards of $953 per minute." This makes Jack a "keeper of secrets." And well, inquisitive minds want to know...

6) Personality-driven: "Renegade"...

7) Story: The entire headline promises that an exciting "story" will be told. Not to mention, the first sentence of the body copy, below the headline reads, "This is a rather unusual story."

When you differentiate yourself and choose, to position yourself as a *Someone*—a celebrity in your marketplace and business community— here's an interesting fact: People *expect* you to be The Most Expensive.

True authorities and celebrities don't come cheap. You don't get Donald Trump for Peewee Herman fees, nor do you expect to.

If you've been to Las Vegas lately and, visited any of the shops in the new hotels, you know you don't walk into Armani or Coach or Gucci and expect to find a $12 suit, shirt or handbag. You know the deal before you step foot in the door. These boutiques are expensive, they don't discount, and just like with a Rolls Royce, the price is what it is. Take it or leave it. You can either afford it, or you're the wrong customer.

Joy perfume, announces in its advertising that, it is the "Costliest Perfume in the World."

What does a high price say about a product or service? What do your fees, if you claim to be the most expensive agent in your marketplace, say about you?

Cheap = Wal-Mart.

Expensive = good.

Expensive = prestigious. Expensive = exclusive.

Just look at Harvard, $61,172.00 a year. (Source: Harvard financial aid and admissions department). There is just one caveat: Price, as a differentiation strategy, must be supported by a true *perceived* difference. In other words, if you allow yourself to just be a clone of the competition, then you can't expect to be paid multiples of what they charge for their products and services.

This is why the 14 Differentiation Strategies discussed in this book, responsible for your positioning, are so critical.

They enable and facilitate inordinately higher profit margins. Same product. Same service. But at a much higher price-point and fee structure!

Any real estate agent and serious entrepreneur can substantially increase their net income if, they commit to "stacking" these Differentiation Strategies, to create a *true* perceived difference, thus, supporting that higher price-point and level of compensation you demand.

That being said, though, how many agents have the courage to lay claim to that title, The Most Expensive Agent in the Marketplace?

Not many.

Relevant Podcast Episodes: 61, 88

<u>**Recommended Resources:**</u>

• **Protector Videos Series** (Access inside Member Site)

• **Case Study Interviews** (Access inside Member Site)

• **AMS Podcast** (www.AMSpodcast.com)

• **Value-Driven Approach** (www.TheValueDrivenApproach.com)

• **Forging Elite Storytellers** (www.StoryAthlete.com)

• **90-Day Immersion** (www.90DayImmersion.com)

• **Explore ImpactClub®** (www.ImpactClub.com)

SOURCE OF
DIFFERENTIATION #13
Marketing Process

By Ryan Fletcher

The majority of ALL business owners, real estate agents and entrepreneurs have no marketing process, only a sales process. And everybody is pretty much taught the same sales process. That is, it's a numbers game. I have a good friend who is single. My wife Melanie says, "He's a dog." The reason she thinks that is because, pretty much, he has the same formula.

It's a numbers game!

There's an old joke about this, I won't bother to tell it. But I will give you the punch line. You ought to know the joke, if not, you can ask someone.

Here's the punch line: "I get slapped a lot, but I get fucked a lot too."

In real estate and in business, this practice of playing the numbers works out pretty much the same. The question becomes: Are you willing to be *that* person? Is that really how you wish to operate your business and make your income—perceived as a "dog?" Where in the minds of prospective clients, they disapprove and do not enjoy your persistent forceful approach?

This is the every "No" is closer to a "yes" method of thinking.

The Guru Party, as I call them, and sales trainers, love to tell you this is what it takes to be successful: Immunity to rejection.

Fine. I agree, you can succeed with brute force and pushing past resistance like a German tank, but consider the effect this "formula" has on your prospective client. You are creating a rude, aggressive, and very uncomfortable and unpleasant experience.

Is this really what you want?

The way I've explained this in the past, "Rapists do not get Valentine's Day cards." So even when you get a "yes," you didn't really get a yes, because you had to use force to get it. Thus, you have damaged, and potentially destroyed, the client's pleasure of buying from you. Even if a woman were to have an orgasm while being raped, although doubtful and unlikely, it doesn't mean she would enjoy it.

Sorry if that is too graphic, but I want to hammer *this* point into your head. Which is:

Society <u>HATES</u> salespeople! So <u>STOP</u> behaving as one!

If working in a niche where people "talk" and where word travels fast, understand, even if just two or three (out of every 100 teachers or nurses, or whatever, you come in contact with) develop a negative opinion about you—word will get out.

Your reputation, your ability to earn trust, will be destroyed.

Warren Buffett has been quoted saying, "If you cost me money, I will forgive you. If you cost me my reputation, I will be ruthless." He did not say, mean, angry, or unforgiving. He said, "Ruthless." This quote speaks volumes to the importance that, the role of reputation plays in business. Your reputation telegraphs to people whether or not you can be trusted—so anything that destroys it is a poor trade.

Good news: There is an alternative to the traditional "sales" process, of persistence and brute force.

By utilizing a sophisticated marketing process, you can differentiate yourself in the mind of prospect clients because, of the different "feelings" they harbor about you vs. your pushy, bossy, and aggressive competitors.

The biggest thing that controls how prospects and clients *feel* about you, is how they were sold—the process by which they came to you and became a client.

Did you chase them? Or did they feel like they were chasing you?

In my business, for example, I wake up almost every morning to fan mail. Not because I'm a true celebrity of any kind—but because I put forth "bait" i.e. free reports, free books, etc. and other *valuable* free information that piques interest, entertains, and compels prospective clients and members to think about their businesses differently.

For this, I am thanked and appreciated.

Also, upon their request, if they are requesting a free report or something, there is a sequence of "conditioning" and "education" that they are put through to pre-sell them, and to differentiate me from any competitors.

If you are a student of Dan Kennedy, you may be familiar with the idea of sequenced mailings: First Notice, Second Notice, Third Notice information packages.

One of the best positioning tools you can use in your business to establish authority—the ultimate *influential* trigger—is a book that you have authored, licensed to author, etc. that demonstrates your authority, knowledge, belief system and unique approach.

At the back of this chapter is an ad for such a book (See Figure 13.1 on page 115). That book, *The VALUE-DRIVEN APPROACH to Sell Real Estate: A practical guide to protect yourself from REAL ESTATE GREED & bank an extra $30,000 by thinking like the great WARREN BUFFETT*, has worked amazingly well for members of my P/SS

program. No longer do they do listing presentations. They don't cold-call. They never experience rejection. And, an added bonus, securing full commissions and transaction fees has become easier than ever. *Why?* This book positions them as a thought-leader to prospective clients.

Remember, when you set out to position yourself as a

"Someone"—and you do it—people have expectations that you will not be cheap, not to mention, have to qualify to work with you.

The book that you are reading now, *Defeat Mega-agents*, in essence, serves the same purpose. Now, if and when I talk to an interested agent or entrepreneur about my programs, on the phone or in person, prior to that person becoming a client or member of mine, the dynamics of the relationship have changed. Having read this book, they understand, at least somewhat, who I am, what I do, and how I am different.

Because I have authored a book, I'm not viewed as a salesperson. I'm seen as the authority on a subject that interests them, and possibly, is the solution to their problem.

If you Google the phrase, "Never talk to anyone, until they know you are a someone," you'll find that this is a trademarked® phrase that I own. But it is more than that. It is how I choose to do business. It is also the premise for what I teach to agents and private clients, about how they too should operate their businesses—from a position of power—people coming to them, not the other way around. I just can't see where there is any honor in being a lowly-respected salesperson. If you must prospect; knock-on doors, cold call, or beg family and friends for referrals, you have, in my opinion, failed up to this point to establish yourself as a true authority and/or as a *Someone*.

The good news, you can always change that.

How important is it to have a sophisticated marketing process?

I suppose it depends on your *personal* goals, about how you wish to conduct business. Do you want to attract clients to you, or...are you all right with having to chase these folks down, then willing to beat them with a club until they yell, "uncle"?

Do you want to be the most expensive agent in your marketplace, or are you all right with working for clients that ask you to cut your fee…and that undermine your authority?

As a direct-response strategist and copywriter, I'm paid fees of $25,000 to $50,000 per project, plus royalties tied to results for private client work. I am certain without a sophisticated marketing process, to effectively position the value of my services, that fee structure would be impossible. Could I be wrong? *Maybe*. But in my experience, when you ask someone to pay you over $1,000 per hour, you better have positioned yourself as a *Someone* to be able to get it.

Similarly, as a consultant, my daily rate is $8,200. My last client (as of writing this) flew in from Toronto, Canada, to Vancouver, WA, to meet with me for just one day to discuss his business and marketing ideas. The next day, he flew home. His total cost to meet with me, well over $10,000.00.

Again, I am certain, without a sophisticated marketing process to effectively position the value of my services, that rate—over $1,000 per hour—would be impossible to obtain.

When I was a pre-med student, I'd heard of orthopedic surgeons and other surgeon types being paid those kinds of fees, but never did I imagine I could be paid those kinds of fees as a marketing consultant. That is, until, I discovered the fourteen *Differentiation Strategies* outlined in this book, and began to implement them.

You defeat Mega-agents, elevate your status, authority, and increase your ability to command larger fees, through the construction of a powerful marketing process. Such a process or protocol that clients must go through, first, before being granted the privilege to speak to you in person, is a profound source of differentiation.

Relevant Podcast Episodes: 3, 19, 29, 36, 75-78, 82-84, 103

<u>Recommended Resources:</u>

• **Protector Videos Series** (Access inside Member Site)

• **Case Study Interviews** (Access inside Member Site)

• **AMS Podcast** (www.AMSpodcast.com)

• **Value-Driven Approach** (www.TheValueDrivenApproach.com)

• **Forging Elite Storytellers** (www.StoryAthlete.com)

• **90-Day Immersion** (www.90DayImmersion.com)

• **Explore ImpactClub®** (www.ImpactClub.com)

FIGURE 13-1: Book ad, full size 8.5 x 11 – one of many ads (within the P/SS program) licensed to P/SS members for promotion.

FIGURE 13-2: A sample of the Trust / Authority article (Page 1 of 3, shown here) that is provided each month to Protector/Social Superhero members. Each Trust / Authority article then makes a direct-response offer for the "Warren Buffett" book – initiating a sophisticated marketing process. Each Trust / Authority article is different and varies in story and in format, to serve a certain purpose.

Ask RYAN FLETCHER

A Student of
Superior Real Estate Approaches

By Ryan Fletcher

■ ASK THE **AUTHOR**

Email your personal-real estate questions to:
Ryan@L_____
Please include
"Ryan Fletcher Q&A"
in the subject line; or fax to
800-604-6501; or mail to
Q&A w/ Ryan Fletcher
Ask The Author
1413 NW Sluman
Vancouver, WA. 98665

Ryan will answer selected questions in this monthly column. Questions that cannot be answered here, space permitting each month, will be answered individually via email or other communication, if specified and preferred.

Ryan Fletcher is the author of the landmark new book, "The Warren Buffett Approach To Sell Real Estate." **A free copy of the book can be obtained by emailing request to:** Ryan@L_____

I am facing a dilemma. I have a family member who is a real estate agent, and would love to use their services—but I am unsure if they are the most qualified. I don't want to hurt their feelings, but I also don't want to lose profit on the sale of my home.

Curtis J.
Vancouver, WA

First, loyalty is important. But in my experience, having researched the difference between superior real estate approaches and inferior real estate approaches, or as I talk about in my new book, *The Warren Buffett Approach to Sell Real Estate*—a price-driven approach vs. the better value-driven approach—the difference in profit you extract/or lose, depending on which approach you use, can be upwards of $30,000 or more.

Loyalty matters. Good friends are loyal. Good family members are loyal. But the secret to financial success, sometimes, is separating the roles and relationship duties of a family member or friend, someone who is willing to help you move, grab a beer with you, or will let you cry on their shoulder, etc. from that of the professional you hire that is capable of getting you the best result. These are judgment calls you must make. In some cases, if your friend or family members are using an inferior approach, are you willing to walkaway from up to $30,000 of additional profit? Maybe you are, to maintain that relationship—even if you're the one who gets the short end of the (financial) stick.

For more of my thoughts regarding this, read Chapter 5 in my forthcoming book, where I explain the value-driven approach and its benefits, that I learned by studying Warren Buffett, the world's greatest investor, and his investment philosophy.

I am considering hiring a stager for my home sale, but don't know if it's worth it. I'm not afraid to spend money to maximize my investment, but I'm on a limited budget and I don't want to spend money frivolously, if it won't help.

Jessica P.
Vancouver, WA

The answer is, it depends—on who you hire and what kind of staging they perform.

Here is a fact: Model homes generate higher profit.

So, why do more real estate agents NOT spend more time, helping their clients make their homes look and show like model homes?

Once buyers can visualize themselves in a home, can see how the layout will work for their family, can feel the openness and the love of the home; you have lowered their resistance to making an offer and, have vastly increased the likelihood of getting a strong offer—not a conditional one with many "contingencies."

When buyers can openly see a house, as their house, not one that is lived in by another family, then the buyer will start—as we want them to—making emotional decisions, not logical ones. This is why home builders, and you may not know this, spend so much time studying the science of staging homes. Scientific staging offers much greater profit potential than conventional staging, as most real estate agents and home stagers push their clients toward.

For my clients, this is why I hire THE BEST, MOST SUCCESSFUL stagers in the area, Stacy and Sharon at Limelight Staged Homes.

Have you ever seen the show *Love It or List It?* If not, it's a simple premise.

First, there is a homeowner. This homeowner, usually, is a person who's grown somewhat bored with their home and now is considering selling it. Then there are the hosts of the show. Interior designer, Hilary Farr, and real estate agent David Visentin – these are the people responsible for the transformation of each home.

While designer Hilary attempts to restore the homeowner's excitement about their home, real estate agent David tries to find the couple the home of their dreams.

Once all work has been complete and all potential homes have been viewed, the couples must decide whether to "love their home" or "list it" – about seventy-percent of the time – the homeowner chooses to "love their home" and keep it rather than sell it

This demonstrates how the proper use of *scientific* staging, can be powerful. And can be a huge motivator in making a buying decision. This works on a behavioral level. Scientific staging pushes buyers from just comparing beds, baths and square footage, to being emotionally connected to a home for which they can see themselves living in—the

FIGURE 13-3: Another example of a Trust / Authority article—provided each month to Protector/Social Superhero members, to establish members as innovators, authors and thought-leaders.

It's not as easy as you think to achieve maximum profit...

True Differentiation:
How it impacts profit and dictates strategy when selling a home.

By Ryan Sloper, author, creator: *The Warren Buffett Approach To Sell Real Estate: A practical guide to protect yourself from REAL ESTATE GREED & bank an extra $30,000 by taking a VALUE-DRIVEN APPROACH.*

I realize the image to the right may look a little Howard Hughes-ish, but there is a method to my madness. And this sketch, if you're thinking of selling your home, may have a profound and direct impact on your bottom-line profit. You'll also want to share this with friends and family members that you care about too.

When I set out to study Warren Buffett, his investment philosophy, to find out what made him the world's greatest investors, and, ultimately, how his methods could be applied to my clients' home sale—I came stumbled upon a book called *Differentiate or Die*. This book changed my entire perspective on real estate. Jack Trout was the author. In the book he laid out the fundamental reasons why a business must differentiate from competitors, not just to be successful, but as the key ingredient to thrive in our current era of *Killer Competition*. Now, admittedly, from a business perspective, this is common sense. Every entrepreneur knows he must differentiate his business. As a mentor once told me, "Nobody needs two left shoes." In business, if two businesses are the same, then one is dispensable.

But, this got me thinking.

Business, and the fight for new customers, really, is no different than real estate and the fight for homebuyers.

Your home is a home, yes, but analogously speaking, it is also product no different than Tide laundry detergent, where you are the owner of that product, no different than Proctor & Gamble is Tide. And see, when you look at your home through this lens—the profit from your home sale; its ability to compete in the marketplace—comes down to your ability to differentiate.

Is your home no different than the many other homes on the market? Is it just a commodity? Or is it different, and could it be judged superior?

In my sketch above, you'll notice there are three scenarios. Each scenario describes the starting position of your product, your home, in relation to other competing homes on the market. Each of these scenarios can also be thought of as a race.

The more and better you differentiate your *product*, the faster you move forward toward higher profit. And of course, the less you differentiate the faster you move backwards toward lower profit. All the while the other homes on the market, in your neighborhood, in your price range, with similar square footage, amenities, etc., are competing in the same race.

In scenario #1 – you, your home, you start even with your competitors. You are neither ahead of behind. There is no discernable difference between your home and others. No apparent advantages and no apparent disadvantages.

In scenario #2 – you, your home, starts out ahead of the competition. This could be for a number reasons. But through some means of differentiation, you have the advantage of a 5-second head start. All the while so long as you run the race appropriately, and don't trip over your feet or make a fundamental mistake, you have increased odds of winning.

In scenario #3 –you, your home, starts out at a notable disadvantage to the competition. You are now the underdog, not the frontrunner. And to win, and bank the most profit from your home sale, you'll have to run the race of your life.

Part of my job then becomes, prior to creating the actual "race strategy," is to determine where a clients' home's starting position is.

If you're running the 800-meter dash, for example, someone running on the inside lanes—from a strategic standpoint—must run a very different race than the runner who runs in the outside lanes. Similarly, the runner with a known disadvantage, like

FIGURE 13-3: Cont'd: Page 2.

Aimee Lee Mullins who I wrote about last month, who set multiple NCAA records despite having her lower legs amputated as a child, must run a very different race than the runner who doesn't have that handicap.

Now you would think that every home, given the three scenarios above, either a) starts out even, b) ahead or c) behind the competition, right? *Wrong.* There is actually a 4th possible scenario.

In scenario #4 – you, your home, starts out ahead of the competition but…only "in your mind." For obvious reasons, this is dangerous.

When a homeowner is blinded to their true starting position in relation to other competing homes on the market; due to pride of ownership, ego, arrogance, lack of understanding of how true differentiation works, how value is created, etc., almost always, in my experience, they sabotage their chance for maximum profit.

There is, by the way, nothing wrong with starting from behind. The fabled underdog story exists for this reason, to upset the odds-makers. But the underdog, to win, must realize he is the underdog and, through strategy, offset his handicap.

David versus Goliath: An apparent mismatch, but in this fight Goliath's size is no match for a small well-placed stone, shot from a distance, out of reach of Goliath, from David's high-tension slingshot. *Bing!* One stone upside the head, and Goliath is out.

This is why, in my book, The Warren Buffett Approach to Sell Real Estate: How to protect yourself from Real Estate Greed and bank an extra $30K in profit by taking a Value-Driven Approach, I talk about the importance of getting an accurate and comprehensive diagnosis—for this very reason—to identify your homes' true starting point.

The last scenario in the world you ever want to participate in is scenario #4.

One interesting tidbit too, about how true differentiation works, when done correctly and effective, you not only control whether your home moves forward or backward "in the race" toward higher or lower profit, you also control whether other competing homes (with yours) move forward or backward too.

I suppose its kind of like cheating, that is tying a rope around your competitor, and anchoring him to a tree before the start of the race, but hey – that other homeowner should have hired someone who understands true differentiation, then they wouldn't have been in that position, chained to a lower potential profit.

The biggest secret, though, for maximum profit, you must know your "product's" starting point in relation to its competitors. Without this, nothing else really matters, as the details are fiction and hypothetical, and not reality.

But with reality, we can get to true strategy.

If it turns out that we're the underdog, so be it, we'll run the race of the underdog and in accord to the facts, to strive for the upset. ∎

For a more in-depth discussion on this topic, go to: ████████████████
There you can request a **FREE** copy of my forthcoming book "The Warren Buffett Approach To Sell Real Estate: How to protect yourself from Real Estate Greed & bank an extra $30K in profit by taking a Value-Driven Approach.

RYAN SLOPER - AUTHOR & CREATOR

An entrepreneur and a relentless innovator of the real estate industry, Ryan Sloper, is the creator of the "Warren Buffet Approach to Sell Real Estate," author of the infamous report, "Frauds, Lies, Cheats & Unethical Scams," he also founded Northern VA's Nurse Only Program®, and is a licensed agent with U.S. Realty Partners. Sloper has been called "provocative and entertaining", but also, "a committed philanthropist" for his mission to raise/donate over $10,000 to local and nurse-related charities each year. Ryan also supports many great national charities too, such as: St. Jude's Children's Hospital, Wounded Warrior Project®, Smile Train®, Susan G. Komen Race for the Cure®, MADD: Mother's Against Drunk Driving among others. Ryan is a leader in the Bristow business community as well, and co-founded ENG (Entrepreneurs Networking Group™) Bristow Chapter—an exclusive group of ambitious business owners and entrepreneurs, focused on three core pillars of impact:
Philanthropy. Business. And growth.

COMMON SENSE DISCLAIMER:

The book: "The Value-Driven Approach To Sell Real Estate: A Practical Guide To Protect Yourself From Real Estate Greed & Bank An Extra $30,000 By Thinking Like The Great Warren Buffett" is NOT in any way officially endorsed, or associated, or recommended by Warren Buffett, himself. The content of the book, and the approach discussed is based solely on the research of Mr. Buffett's very *public* and very well-known investment philosophy; published in articles, books, interviews, etc. All views and opinions present in the book, are in no way representative of Mr. Buffett or any of his associated companies.

FOURTEEN

SOURCE OF
DIFFERENTIATION #14
Leadership Position

By Ryan Fletcher

What makes a company or individual strong is not the product or service. It's the position it *owns* in the mind of the prospect. Author Al Ries, in his book *22 Immutable Laws* speaks to the importance of being the leader in your category, saying, paraphrased, "If you can't be #1 in your prospects' mind— the leader in your category; business, product or service—create a new bucket for which you can be the leader."

When Steve Jobs launched the iPod, iPhone, and then the iPad, they were all first-of-their-kind products. By virtue of being first, Apple became the leader and, assumed leader, in each of these product categories, where, the terms: iPhone, iPod or iPad have become the accepted generic term for all personal music devices, smart phones and tablets. Kind of like Kleenex, it's a brand, but it's also the generic term for all kinds of tissue.

145

Once you *own* a position in the mind of a prospect, it really is yours to lose.

A survey of 25 leading brands from the year 1923 forward, proves this point. Today, 21 of those brands are still in first place. Three are in second place, and one is in fifth place. What's this mean? It means, if you're able to successfully create a "new bucket" or, at least, the perception of having created a "new bucket," for your business, product or service, and, you effectively market and position that new bucket as *belonging* to you, and your business, then, for years to come, you are likely to have a differentiating advantage.

How is this done? I'll give you an example.

Working with members of my Protector/Social Superhero program, I launched ENG: Entrepreneurs Networking Group™—a by-application-only-community for ambitious business owners and entrepreneurs to discuss high-level marketing, positioning and differentiation strategies. Using a sophisticated marketing process (Differentiation Strategy # 13), each agent-member is positioned as the co-founder of their local branch (See Figure 14.1 on page 127.)

In the first week, we opened 28 branch locations across the United States and Canada, making it the fastest growing networking group of its kind.

The Secret—is how ENG is positioned.

ENG is not like other "networking" or "leads" groups. No one begs for referrals. This is not a group for the uninitiated masses. Our local groups are different. Our marketing message *only* speaks to a certain kind of business owner, and that business owner or entrepreneur, must apply to be accepted, much like the mastermind group I told you about, previously, that my friend joined at fee of $25,000 per year. Except, ENG is free. The purpose of each ENG Chapter is not to make money by selling memberships. It's purpose is to serve as *the vehicle* that enables members of my Protector/Social Superhero program to build a large referral network for their real estate services.

We call this concept: *Organizing an Army*. In fact, using this concept, P/SS member Trish Yocum went from ZERO to nearly 3-million in production—in a marketplace that averages less than $140K per home—in just 8 months. That equates to 27 transactions. Since then, she has started a second ENG group and, at the time of this writing, just halfway through the calendar year, has already surpassed her previous years' production and income levels.

Further, if you look carefully at how most networking groups operate. Most of these groups are filled with *unsuccessful* business owners and entrepreneurs, where each group-member begs each other for business and referrals. And, as an aside, publicly-begging-for-business kills your authority. But from what I can tell, this game they play seems to be about whom can hand out the most business cards and/or give the most elevator speeches.

I call it, "Human Spamming."

But by initiating an application process, where interested business owners must apply, and then, by *only* accepting the serious entrepreneurs, you attract a different fish. Thus, we have created a "new bucket" because, previously, that *successful* fish would never have been interested in joining any networking or leads group that would be filled with, or require them to associate with, human-spammers.

In short (Differentiation Strategy No. 2), we have created a new *place* for the *successful* business owner to belong.

Something I have always said, "There are two types of people. There are people who drink Scotch. And there are people who drink Pabst. Rarely do they hang out together or at the same place."

ENG: Entrepreneurs Networking Group™ is for the *serious* business owner and entrepreneur—the *only* kind of businessperson we like and, that is worth associating yourself with for strategic purpose.

Being the original 'known' pioneer of a great idea, movement, concept, program, service, accomplishment, or place— differentiates you from the generic, same as everyone else competition.

Vince Lombardi was the first NFL coach to win the Super Bowl. That trophy, today, still bares his name: *The Lombardi Trophy.*

This phenomenon is true for more business examples than I could possibly cover in 100 more pages. So I won't. But that doesn't diminish the importance or effectiveness of *being* first—to market—with a product, service or idea.

True differentiation is the ownership of *that* place in the mind of your prospect. When they think of X, they think of you, your business or service. That's the ultimate endgame you achieve [and enjoy] when you implement into your business the 14 *Differentiation Strategies* discussed in this book. And, when you do. Mega-agents…

They're dead.

Relevant Podcast Episodes: 15, 17, 24, 25, 59, 60, 89, 100, 102, 104

Recommended Resources:

• *Protector Videos Series* (Access inside Member Site)

• **Case Study Interviews** (Access inside Member Site)

• **AMS Podcast** (www.AMSpodcast.com)

• **Value-Driven Approach** (www.TheValueDrivenApproach.com)

• **Forging Elite Storytellers** (www.StoryAthlete.com)

• **90-Day Immersion** (www.90DayImmersion.com)

• **Explore ImpactClub®** (www.ImpactClub.com)

FIGURE 14-1: ENG co-Founder sites, Peoria vs. Bristow

FIGURE 14-2: Cheryl Gordon's ENG Ad (ran in her newsletter) – that led to 11 new member applications in a week.

FIGURE 14-3: Sample of a typical ENG application – from a business owner/entrepreneur seeking acceptance into a local ENG chapter.

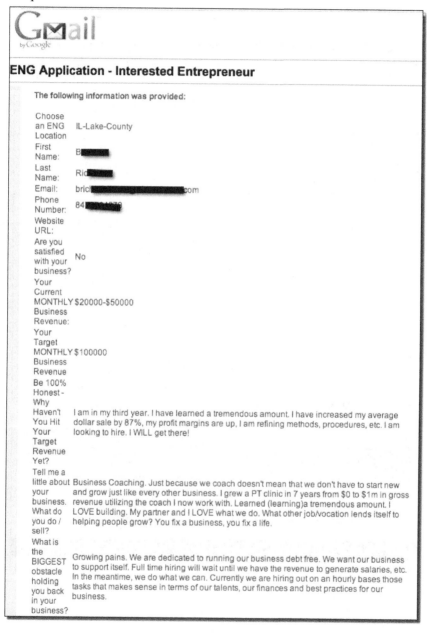

ENG Application - Interested Entrepreneur

The following information was provided:

Choose an ENG Location	IL-Lake-County
First Name:	B███████
Last Name:	Ric███████
Email:	bric███████com
Phone Number:	84███████
Website URL:	
Are you satisfied with your business?	No
Your Current MONTHLY Business Revenue:	$20000-$50000
Your Target MONTHLY Business Revenue	$100000
Be 100% Honest - Why Haven't You Hit Your Target Revenue Yet?	I am in my third year. I have learned a tremendous amount. I have increased my average dollar sale by 87%, my profit margins are up, I am refining methods, procedures, etc. I am looking to hire. I WILL get there!
Tell me a little about your business. What do you do / sell?	Business Coaching. Just because we coach doesn't mean that we don't have to start new and grow just like every other business. I grew a PT clinic in 7 years from $0 to $1m in gross revenue utilizing the coach I now work with. Learned (learning)a tremendous amount. I LOVE building. My partner and I LOVE what we do. What other job/vocation lends itself to helping people grow? You fix a business, you fix a life.
What is the BIGGEST obstacle holding you back in your business?	Growing pains. We are dedicated to running our business debt free. We want our business to support itself. Full time hiring will wait until we have the revenue to generate salaries, etc. In the meantime, we do what we can. Currently we are hiring out on an hourly bases those tasks that makes sense in terms of our talents, our finances and best practices for our business.

FIGURE 14-3: Cont'd

What changes need to be made to reach your revenue goals?	We need to continue lead generation in our Target Market, Hire Coaches, Hire Staff, increase our Average Dollar Sale, Improve our Closing percentages, and continue learning, refining, improving and growing both personally and professionally so we can better guide and educate our clients. Accountability is a two way street.
Do you run an ethical business?	Yes
Are you a team player? / Can you be trusted?	Yes
Why do you have an interest in joining this group?	Disenchanted with BNI, etc. I am an active member with good participation. I am part of a club that produces over $1 m in revenue each year, however, we are missing the point. I saw the video and it fits with my thoughts. I have always held the philosophy that if I do the best job that I can for the people who I serve, the money will come. I want to be surrounded by Like-Minded folks. We have a following of 40-60 Business Owners who attend our Complimentary Seminars (we believe it is important to give back to the community that supports us). We are building a Community of Like-Minded Business Owners. People to grow with, learn with, do business with and refer to. People we can trust. People we know will deliver. People with follow through. People who we can help and we can look to for help.
Could you handle an influx of new clients?	Yes
Is your belief system "in sync" w/ the ENG belief system?	Yes
If accepted, what skills / benefits / value do you bring to the group?	A former Business Executive from Corporate America, MBA with loads of experience in every facet of business who has owned several businesses of his own. One of which he was an interim CEO for companies that were between CEO's. Great exposure to many industries and cultures. Long story short, he had a calling and he left everything to fulfill it. He wanted to help the Small Business Owner reach higher levels through training, mentorship and accountability. Not just to make them more money, but to change their lives. Help them reach their legacy. Help them make an impact on the world. I hired this Coach when I owned the PT clinic. He shared my philosophy of life and faith and taught me all about my numbers which was the missing component for me. Once I had a grasp of my cost of sales, my margins, break evens, average dollar sales... I moved forward very quickly. My Business Partner, at the time, did not share my philanthropic mentality, so I sold my shares to her and joined my Coach's Team. Now, I have the privilege of helping other folks reach heights they only dreamed about. The video is spot on—profits put us in a position of choice. I have a legacy (a dream) of opening a leadership institute for young adults. I have five children of my own. I want our future leaders to have a place to learn how to really function in a world that does not count on entitlement. I am a product of Corporate America, I am a Motivational Speaker, I started and grew a business to $1m gross revenues in 7 years time, and now I am working with a team of Business Coaches to give others what I was given. I get to play it forward—pretty awesome!
If accepted, would you make the weekly meeting a priority?	Yes
When are you looking to get started?	ASAP

FIGURE 14-4: Typical feedback from business owners/entrepreneurs who are accepted to ENG. Needless to say, these kinds of ENG members make for great referral partners.

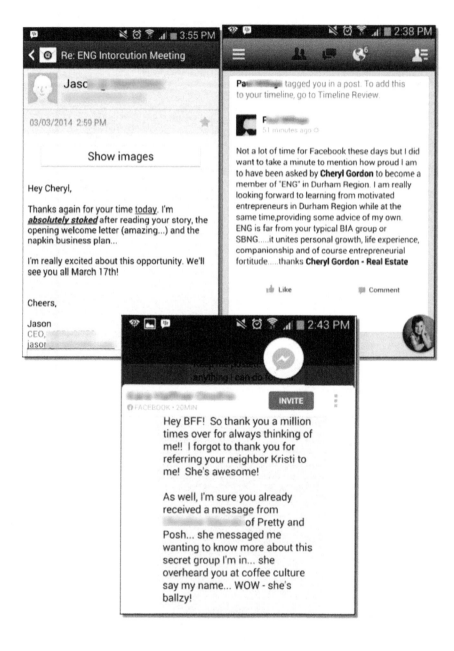

A MEDIA
COMPANY
+
IMPACTCLUB®
=
GAME OVER

FIFTEEN

AMPLIFIER STRATEGY
DELINK AND DISCONNECT
Launch A Media Company

By Ryan Fletcher

M any agents will reject the next statement because it's counterintuitive. Listen to it, though. Hear it, pay attention to it, consider it, then you can decide if you want to reject it: "The absolute *worst* way to grow a real estate business is to *try* to grow the real estate business."

What?!? You heard me. Because the more your focus on the real estate business, again, listen close. "The more you sound like a real estate agent." Which, from a reputation standpoint—a negative reputation, nonetheless, and how stereotypes work—that is a very bad thing. Society does not like real estate agents. Hell, real estate agents don't even like real estate agents. The Unethicals. The Incompetents.

Real estate is one of the few industries on earth, where the people in the industry, actually *hate* their own kind.

Just think. How many agents have you bailed out, during a transaction, when they screwed up? Dropped the ball? Acted unethical? Or were just flat-out incompetent? If you're like most, and if you're honest—that answer is plenty. Likely too many to count.

In my experience, there are three *primary* reasons why someone chooses to get started in real estate. The first category—because it was in their blood. Their mother or father was an agent. Their grandfather was an agent. And they followed in their footsteps. The second category? Since the barrier-of-entry into real estate is so low, and since you can get a real estate license in just a few weeks' time, for only a few hundred bucks, they figured, *"Eh, why not..."* Which, that attitude, also matches their level of professionalism. Leading to a lot of hobbyists in the industry, as well as a heightened number of incompetents.

The third category? This is the one that's most interesting. Almost 73%, according to a recent poll, said they got started in real estate because of a *Horror* Story with their own agent. An experience so awful, when they were buying or selling their own home, they said to themselves, "If that agent of mine who is so terrible, can make that kind of money doing a shitty job – imagine the fortune I could make by doing a good job?"

Which means, when you think about that.

It's astounding.

Real Estate is one of the few industries on earth, where the growth of the industry and the number of new agents getting licensed on a daily, weekly and yearly basis, is actually driven by poor performance. To a large extent, like I said, we actually hate our own kind. And arguably, appropriately so.

Here Are Some FACTS about this:

FACT: The public—your prospective clients—most seem to hate real estate agents too. For the 7th year in a row, according to the Harris Poll's® list of respected professions. Real estate agents have ranked dead last, below even stockbrokers—raising serious questions about their ability to be trusted.

FACT: According to the Gallup Poll's® Honesty and Ethics survey, of those polled, 80% said they did not highly trust real estate agents.

FACT: in a recent Reader's Digest® survey of trusted professions, real estate agents ranked 42 out of 45 listed professions, ahead of only politicians, telemarketers, and car salespeople—three of the LEAST-liked, LEAST-respected, LEAST-trusted professions in the world.

FACT: and, it's undeniable, real estate agents have a very Negative Reputation. Even those agents, like, presumably you, who are good people and honest. Who have ethics, and act with integrity—are viewed poorly (as salespeople and pests) by the public. Why? Because your reputation i.e. that of the "real estate agent" has been destroyed by the vast number of desperate, unethical agents in this industry (their lies and deceit) doing harm to clients, causing them *Horror* Stories.

Here is another FACT: because of the way reputation works, you get pigeon-holed into the Negative Reputation of those *same* desperate, unethical agents. So, by stereotype and snap judgment, you are seen as "one of them" meaning, by prospects...

YOU ARE HATED BEFORE YOU ARRIVE. DISTRUSTED BEFORE YOU SPEAK A WORD

As I stated in a previous chapter, The Oracle from Omaha, Warren Buffett has been quoted, saying, "If you cost me money, I will forgive you. If you cost me my reputation, I will be ruthless." He did not say angry, mad, or unforgiving. He said RUTHLESS.

Most people underestimate just how much "our reputation" rules our life without us even knowing it. You get stereotyped based on your reputation. In other words, your reputation precedes you. It's how others judge you, before they know you.

Reputation is an unspoken language.

In its purest and most powerful form, it's a language based entirely on sight and beliefs. It dictates how you're perceived. Whether you can be trusted (just think how politicians are perceived—can they be trusted?) Your reputation dictates your power, your influence, your authority; even to the extent others respect you. It's not until you understand how reputation works, that you can master it.

EMPOWERING Reputation vs. NEGATIVE Reputation.

The latter one causes you to fail, be miserable, get rejected—no matter how hard you work, or for how long. The other makes success in business almost effortless. And extremely enjoyable. Because people want to do business with you. Want to be associated with you. They trust you. They want to partner with you.

They tell their family and friends about you too, and share with others how they know you. And about what you're an expert at.

The failure to understand this, is why so many business owners, entrepreneurs, and real estate agents fail, when operating in a Negative Reputation industry. Because they never escape the negative stereotype created by the average provider—The Incompetents, The Unethicals—in that industry. Then, when they come into the industry, thinking they will be welcomed with open arms, as the hero, for being the person who cares. Who is competent. Who is ethical. They are met with a very different reality. "No, but I swear. I'm different." "I'm not like them." "I actually care about my clients." But society says, "You look like a duck. You sound like a duck. Thus, you must be a duck—because you have all same markings, due to your training and how you market yourself, as the other seventy-five "real estate agents" who came before you."

And guess what?

They all said those same things too—talking about how different they were as well.

So, truly, if you want to change that *narrative* that says, "You're a real estate agent, no different than all the other real estate *salespeople* out there." Then you must, first, delink and disconnect from that Negative Reputation of the profession. Which, as a by-product, delinks and disconnects you from the negative stereotype.

Next, you must create and control a new *Narrative*. This is your OPN: Own Personal Narrative. We've talked about this at-depth on the podcast. Listen to Ep 62-65.

OPN is the *Narrative* that you Build. Control. Dictate.

It is not the negative one you are given (as an agent) due to the stereotype of the industry. And the kicker? To do this, you have to stop positioning yourself as a "real estate agent." Said different, you have to shed your real estate skin. Get rid of your real estate website. Get rid of your real estate business card. Get rid of your real estate scripts. Get rid of all the "symbols" that society could use, to link you back to one of those dreaded "real estate agents." At all cost, you have to get their wretched *stink* off of you, so it doesn't taint you.

I told you, this is a counterintuitive approach to grow a real estate business. Which is why it's rejected by so many, despite its unparalleled effectiveness.

Here's the story.

Eric Verdi, who I mentioned back in Chapter 6, one day came to me. It was a phone call. "Fletch, people still see me as a real estate agent" he says. I'm thinking about running an ad, in a neighborhood magazine where I want to do more business. I think it will help to change that image of me, what do you think?"

"How much is the ad?" I said. "It varies," he said "depends on the size of the ad, and for how long you want to run it." I said, "ballpark?"

He said "I got it right here… $370 for a quarter page." He then looked up the minimum required contract. "And that's for a 3-month minimum," he says.

My next question, "How big is the neighborhood? In other words, how many people is this magazine being mailed to?"

He says, "Oh, not very many. Maybe 500…"

I said to him, "Out of curiosity, how many ads are in that magazine?" He started flipping through the pages, I could hear him mumbling, counting under his breathe. One, two, ten, twenty-seven, twenty-eight… fifty, fifty-one, two… sixty, sixty-four… "Maybe seventy" he says. And that, my friend, is all I needed to hear.

I said, "Fuck it, we're creating our own magazine."

From having published *Broken Industry* the previous two years, I knew how cheap a magazine could be produced. And to mail it to 500 homes—was dirt cheap too. Especially, when I did that math. Seventy ads times $370 per ad. Ballpark, that's $28,000/month in revenue. Of course, his next question was, "how are we going to create all the content?" I explained to him. Because I had knowledge too, from producing my own podcast, that we would create a local podcast and use guests' interviews as our source of content. We interview them. We get the interviews transcribed. We'd then hire a writer to turn the meat of those transcripts into articles. Boom! That simple. We have magazine content.

And what started as that simple idea. Over the next few years, became a beast.

Taking that basic premise, I then expanded it and devised an entire Media Company concept, complete with multiple monetization paths. And I trademarked the "AdviceGivers®" concept. We had so much invested in it at this point, we wanted to be sure to protect it. You never want copycats or thieves, to blatantly steal your positioning. If they do, you want legal recourse to protect your intellectual property. These are things most business owners, entrepreneurs or agents don't think about, when operating a service. (In real estate, though, especially, copycats and thieves run amuck!! Once something starts working for one, and others see it. Everyone starts copying it.)

Soon, we started launching and testing the "AdviceGivers®" concept nationwide. Launching Media Companies in local markets, as the front-end business to drive the back-end real estate business. The affect was incredible. Real estate agents were no longer seen as "real estate agents." They were Podcast hosts. They were the Editor-in-Chief of magazines. And other local business owners, entrepreneurs and thought-leaders were eager to be associated with them. In a two year span, doing a weekly podcast, Eric quickly interviewed over 120 guests. (See Figure 15.1 on page 142)

Others followed.

Kevin Evers in Wisconsin, another member of the Protector/Social Superhero Program, launched Fox Cities Advice Givers®. Using the same Media Company concept, he quickly interviewed more than 50 local business owners. (See Figure 15.2 on page 143). Creating genuine relationships that connected to, and embedded him in the community. Tim "Spartan" Murphy joined in too, launching Edina SW-MPLS AdviceGivers®. He was the first to add a significant video component to the mix (See Figure 15.3 on page 144), a practice other members quickly adopted, including Sloper and I, in our media company Northern VA AdviceGivers® (See Figure 15.4 on page 144). And this continued. One P/SS member after another, launching "AdviceGivers®" in their local market. Like Jay Lieberman, in Conejo Valley, CA. who's now interviewed more than 100 local guests.

And like Jay, many others have discovered—the power of this model, using a Media Company on the front-end, to forge new relationships, which then drives back-end referrals—is that no one judges you anymore by the negative reputation of the "real estate agent." That negative stereotype no longer haunts you, because now you're a media personality. Not a real estate agent. You're behind the microphone. Which is, for many reasons, an authoritative position.

This is how you Defeat Mega-Agents.

Counterintuitive? Yes.

But this is how one escapes the Negative Reputation and the destructive stereotype of the industry. You stop trying to grow the real estate business, by focusing on the real estate business. You delink and disconnect. You shed your real estate skin. Then you create (and control) your OPN: Own Personal Narrative through the positioning achieved, and content produced, and the new relationships forged, thanks to having built the front-end Media Company. And, to grow a real estate business by any other means, in my opinion, is just plain stupid. For the full argument of what I believe that is true. Listen to Ep 82-84 of the podcast.

Further, building a Media Company is an amplifier strategy—that amplifies the effectiveness of each of the previous 14 Sources of Differentiation. After all, what good is crafting a powerful message, without an equally powerful distribution method?

Which gets to the formula: Front-end media company to power back-end real estate business = Defeat Mega Agents. Because you have *superior* positioning *and* distribution.

Relevant Podcast Episodes: 3, 10, 19, 27, 30, 32, 36, 37, 45, 55, 82-84

Interviews: Eric Verdi, Ryan France, Tim Murphy, Carl Slade, Kevin Evers

<u>Recommended Resources:</u>

• ***Protector Videos Series*** (Access inside Member Site)

- **Case Study Interviews** (Access inside Member Site)

- **AMS Podcast** (www.AMSpodcast.com)

- **Value-Driven Approach** (www.TheValueDrivenApproach.com)

- **Forging Elite Storytellers** (www.StoryAthlete.com)

- **90-Day Immersion** (www.90DayImmersion.com)

- **Explore ImpactClub®** (www.ImpactClub.com)

FIGURE 15-1 and 15-2: Eric Verdi (Frederick) and Kevin Evers (Fox Cities)—a look at their Advice Givers® Media Sites. (Legal: Advice Givers® is a registered trademark and licensed for use to P/SS program members).

FIGURE 15-3 and 15-4: Tim Murphy (left), indicated by the arrow, has worked video into his mix. Ryan Sloper and I, in Northern VA Advice Givers® quickly moved to that higher standard. Creating for featured guests a vast bank of marketing content to be used in their business for promotional purpose.

FIGURE 15-5: In addition to podcast, articles, video content, etc. below is a look at the magazine that Advice Givers® Media Companies create too—for distribution to Show Partners. The Magazine is powerful demonstration of Differentiation Strategy No. 1, 5, 7, 8, 9, 10, 13 and 14.

SIXTEEN

AMPLIFIER STRATEGY
INSPIRE THE UNINSPIRED
Birth Of ImpactClub®

By Ryan Fletcher

There comes a time when you're ready and capable to lead a much bigger mission. Your life's purpose is not to be real estate agent. I'm guessing you feel "called" to be something much more. Like Bill Gates and Rockefeller did, and other great entrepreneurs, there exists a shift toward impacting others.

Stepping up, becoming the leader. Inspiring others. Making a difference. Passing on principles and beliefs. Leading an army who think and believe like you do. Who also want to make a difference, but don't know. Becoming a philanthropist on a much larger scale. Bringing people together, to belong to something bigger...

If you didn't, I doubt you'd be reading this book. And I say that, because I have learned about the readers of this book, by working with the readers who came before you.

Funded by successful businesses. Fulfilled by impacting lives.

In this Chapter, what you're about to read is how 15 agents who dared to believe they could be more than just real estate agents, birthed a local movement in their community.

People came together. They believed. In fact, in just the first 18-months, more than $1.4 million in already donated, or to be donated funds, have been secured to impact local charities.

In the process, these agents, who have become Conscious Capitalists, have become well-recognized leaders in their communities. They have escaped negative reputation. And built an empowering reputation, through being a leader.

ImpactClub® Origins: (ImpactClub.com)

In the book *The Upstarts* by Brad Stone, detailing the rise of companies like Airbnb and Uber, he writes, "Every company creates its own origin myth. It's a useful tool for expressing the company's values to employees and the world, and for simplifying, and messaging history to give due-credit to the people who made the most important contribution(s) back when it all started…"

He then makes the point.

"Most of the myths are exaggerated, true in direction. But with creative license in terms of the details." That said, personally, I care not to exaggerate. Nor do I need any creative license.

When it comes to ImpactClub®, on our website (ImpactClub.com) you can watch the exact vision, just as I laid it at the feet of my entrepreneurial friends – other agents like you, who become Conscious Capitalists – that day in Orlando back in 2016. Hurricane Matthew raged outside, while I walked through the details.

How ImpactClub® could be built, and how it could be amplified, and how, within a decade, it could be one of the most effective brands in the world, donating hundreds of millions to local charities.

ImpactClub® was Born Out of a Frustration!

This is what we learned.

People want to do more to impact the lives of others, but they don't know how. This was especially true for me, and this group of entrepreneurs I worked with. Each had a successful business, from having purchased this book, and implementing the differentiation strategies. But something was missing.

And I wasn't the only one to feel it. Income wise, business was good. It was good for all of us.

The fulfillment, though, wasn't there.

As a group, we started to ponder such questions: Why were we all fighting so hard to grow our business, what was the bigger purpose? There has to be something beyond just more customers, clients, users, and beyond just making more money?

What's next?...

Around that time, the concept of a giving circle was introduced to me and the agents I was working with. It wasn't the first time I had heard of the concept. But it was the first time that it clicked. This led everyone, including me, to do a mountain of research. Could the giving group model be improved?

Without even trying, we found holes and shortcomings in every version we analyzed. Everything from being highly-inefficient to being just flat out broken. Most were run as "hobby-projects," oppose to the precision of a true organization. So in the true spirit of

Elon Musk, just as he did when designing Tesla and SpaceX, and Solar City, we dared to start with a clean slate.

Innovation Isn't Free.

By the time I mapped out the entire vision of what we would build, and how all its components would integrate (from the infrastructure of ImpactClub®, the Sport of Elevated Philanthropy, to the Leaderboards, and all the tech needed for IOD: Impact of the Day, for tracking and rewards) to make it possible. We landed on a figure that was north of $300,000 to build the needed infrastructure. Not to mention, the cost of video production, hiring videographers. Post production. Investing in data and video systems. Travel to and from events. Plus, the cost of launching in each new city itself.

Using the capital from our other companies, Ryan Sloper and I, my business partner, vowed to put up the money to build the national infrastructure, if… each local entrepreneur, as they became skilled-enough storytellers (Level 1, Level 2 Certified) would fund the ongoing cost to launch a local ImpactClub® in their community.

It Was Unanimous, Each Agreed

The next month, in November of 2016, I hired the tech team that is responsible for having brought ImpactClub® to life.

On December 19th, a month after our tech team investment, to begin testing our concept, ImpactClub® Northern VA launched. In just one hour on that night, from 112 founding ImpactClub® members, a huge check for $11,200 was donated to ImpactClub's first recipient - StillBrave: Childhood Cancer Foundation.

A month after that, on January 28th, ImpactClub® Temecula launched. Taking what we learned from the first launch (the power of Open-Source Learning) and applying it – we grew first-event-member-count from 112 Impact Venture Capitalists to 181. Where in doing so, in just one hour, those members donated $18,100 to an incredible local charity.

A month later on March 28th, this again repeated in Frederick, Maryland. Where, thanks to 182 ImpactClub® members, a check for $18,200 was donated to another incredible local charity, helping to fund the fight against domestic abuse.

As They Say, "The Rest is History!"

What we built, caught wind...

Each member became an evangelist, all too happy and eager to spread the message.

You see, this is the power of story.

A story is not just words on a piece of paper. A story is a carefully crafted message intended to build an Army of support for a business, cause, or purpose.

"To Inspire the Uninspired."

"To Be the Strongest Community in Every Community!"

And it's our members fanatical commitment to those things that make our members different most other people I've ever stumbled upon. They don't say "they care" because that's what they're supposed to say. Or because it's popular. They say it because they actually care, and each day, by their actions, choose to demonstrate it.

Our Creed: "You can count on me!"

The best part?

ImpactClub® is a diverse group of members, made up of the five dominant Character Types:

1 - Growth Hackers
2 - Conscious Capitalists
3 - Charitable Founders
4 - Affected family members
And 5 - The Connector.

"These are my people. This is home."

I've heard that sentiment too many times to count, especially from new members after attending their first event. The sense of belonging. Camaraderie. Knowing that others share their same character-beliefs and values.

"The Strongest Community in Every Community™"

Our members make that true.

As storytellers and Impact Venture Capitalists they invest in their community.

And to think, ImpactClub® was launched and funded, and made possible, by myself, Sloper, and thanks to group of "real estate agents" who became Conscious Capitalists, because they dared to believe they could be something more.

They stopped focusing on leads and sales. And started living by a simple code: Connect. Inspire. Create. You don't Defeat Mega-

Agents by playing the same game. As I said in the Introduction of this book:

"When you sell a commodity, which is what most products are, which are what most professional services are, where the perception is that you, and every service-provider in that industry, i.e. real estate, do the exact same thing and/or sell the exact same product—your challenge is to find a way to change the rules of the game so you appear different from competitors—even if you sell, fundamentally, the same product or offer the exact same service. In other words, if you can't alter the product or service to gain a competitive advantage, you must alter something else."

And it is my hope, over these last 16 chapters, I have demonstrated and given you a Playbook of exactly how to do that. My ImpactClub® cofounders became master *Storytellers!*

That is their Secret.

That is how they Defeat Mega-Agents.

That is how they became A Someone.

And that is how they earned the right to become a Cofounder, to launch an ImpactClub® in their local market – impacting hundreds of lives, raising tens to hundreds of thousands for local charities, and, all in all, became the Leader of their local movement.

Level 1, 2, 3 Storyteller = Conscious Capitalist = Heroic Purpose! Connect. Inspire. Create. Or said different: Content. Distribution. Scale & Impact.

Relevant Podcast Episodes: 85, 95, 97, 98, 100, 101, 102, 103, 104

Interviews: Robert Grand, Josh Painter, Kevin Evers

Recommended Resources:

• **Protector Videos Series** (Access inside Member Site)

• **Case Study Interviews** (Access inside Member Site)

• **AMS Podcast** (www.AMSpodcast.com)

• **Value-Driven Approach** (www.TheValueDrivenApproach.com)

• **Forging Elite Storytellers** (www.StoryAthlete.com)

• **90-Day Immersion** (www.90DayImmersion.com)

• **Explore ImpactClub®** (www.ImpactClub.com)

FOR REAL ESTATE AGENTS
WHO WANT TO BE
SOMETHING
MORE
THAN JUST
"REAL ESTATE AGENTS!"

SEVENTEEN

ASK YOURSELF
THIS QUESTION
"What is my purpose?"

By Ryan Fletcher

I t's not something most people do. Most people, I think, never really consider, much less ask, and then really probe into the question: *What is my purpose?*

Maybe the answer is one they don't care about, or, maybe they've never thought to ask the question. Or maybe "having a purpose," they think, is reserved for other, more special, more important people—but not them. I have a cousin, in fact, several cousins who I believe fall into that latter category, of not feeling worthy of a purpose. One, a sophomore in high school. She wants to be a teacher, but doesn't believe it's possible—at least—not for her. I've often wondered, is this an issue with her self-confidence? Maybe she doesn't have any sense of self-worth. Or maybe she doesn't think she's smart enough to go to college, or, for another reason, doesn't believe she is capable? Maybe for money reasons or because of the low-expectations impressed upon her by others; family, friends, etc.

I suspect it's a "mix" of each.

I have another cousin who just graduated high-school last year. He wants to be a marine biologist. But, it took me two hours of probing to get him to admit that. For two hours, I asked, "What do you want to do with your life? What do you want to be?" And for two hours he said, "I don't know. Leave me alone," to which I said, "bullshit." *He knew.* He knew damn well what he wanted to be. But then again, knowing, and becoming, are two entirely different feats. He was afraid to say what he really wanted to be in life. He feared sounding stupid. Thinking people would laugh at him for wanting something, in his mind, "so preposterous."

On the other hand, my little man Jackson a.k.a. "Bruce Wayne/Batman" believes in his heart-of-hearts, when he turns five, that he'll board a plane and finally visit the city he's read so much about: *Gotham.* He never fears feeling stupid. (By the way, five is a big year for Jackson. He basically has it all planned out, he will rule the world when he turns five.) Maybe he's right. I don't know. I'm not a prophet nor do I control anyone's destiny. And who am I to tell him he can't or won't—maybe he will.

In terms of achieving success, there's simply no replacement for that kind of confidence, and it's a confidence we're all born with. It's only later that society beats out of us. And regardless of the set of tools or strategies, or even the best advice in the world. Nothing can fill the void in a person whose been "taught" to lack confidence in himself or feels unworthy, or incapable, because someone has told him repeatedly, over and over again that something isn't possible.

And truth told. Maybe it is possible.

Maybe, someday, Jackson will visit Gotham City. Not physically, but metaphorically. There is an excellent book, "The Boy Who Loved Batman," authored by Michael Uslan, who produced the most recent Batman trilogy. By age 9, he owned thousands of comic books, by age 12, he was writing his own comic stories, and while still in his twenties, secured the film rights to Batman. Over a decade later, Uslan brought "his version" of Batman, The Dark Knight to the silver screen—with collective box office revenues, totaling nearly $2.5 billion.

You could argue Michael Uslan "visited" Gotham City. He built movie sets the size of New York city blocks. You could argue his success has made him ruler of his "own" world. You could argue his childhood fantasy, due to his own perseverance and willingness to believe in the impossible, became his adult reality.

I'm certainly not going to tell Jackson he can't do the same. It's not my place or my right to squash dreams.

But that doesn't answer the question, "What is my purpose?"

This is a question I've asked a lot lately. I believe as a parent, as a friend, as a mentor, as a consultant, as whatever "title" you wish to give me or others assign me—I believe my purpose is to inspire. To lift up and encourage others to dream. To think big. And not just big. But huge. To not be afraid to imagine the impossible. To keep hope alive and not be fearful of the unknown. To not be cowardly in times when courage is needed. To step up when others won't. I believe my purpose is to help others to un-cork and un-bottle, to un-lock the potential locked inside themselves. I believe my purpose is to help others expand their vision to see what is *actually* possible and not just what society tells us is possible. I believe my purpose is to help others create their own destiny and to fulfill their own mission.

Of course, getting to this point has not been easy. For most of my life, I have felt like an outcast. Not in the traditional sense, and I don't mean in high school. Rather in my work and professional life. When you set your alarm to wake up every morning at 4:00am, write

7 days a week, on holidays and even vacations—several thoughts move through people's minds: 1) He must be crazy, and 2) he must be a workaholic.

When you ask for, and only want books for Christmas, people assume you're a boring dud. When you spend 99% of your time writing, alone by yourself, it is assumed you don't have any friends or, they say assume that you're "disconnected and shut-off." They say things like, "I guess I'm more of a people-person. I could never do what you do," as if to suggest that I'm some version of Howard Hughes—who late in his life never ventured out, never cut his finger nails, and shut himself off completely from the outside world. They're also quick to call you a "sucker" when you spend $5,000 to attend a marketing seminar. They say things like "I thought you were smarter than that," or "I didn't think you would fall for something like that." And when you shoot videos of yourself and post them on the Internet for all the world to see, you're labeled and called a narcissist.

While I've come to accept these "titles" and "classifications" that others have for me.

I'm really only one thing: A *Storyteller.*

When I look back at the body of work I've created. At my marketing. At my content. At the way I present my unique perspective on marketing and advertising, in my newsletters and in my videos. When I look at the sales letters I've written. Ads I've written. At the way I present my philosophy and beliefs; about business, success, and about the elements required to create a movement...

What I find: Are *stories.*

In a recent conversation with a member of my Protector / Social Superhero program, I received, jokingly, what I consider the greatest compliment of my career. Her comment to me, "You're like the Jesus of Marketing." And while it may sound horribly arrogant and conceited of me to accept any comparison to Jesus, it's not for egotistical reasons. I am no Jesus. I know that. And she didn't make the comment suggesting any such "real" comparison. Our conversation was about the power of story. Jesus was a storyteller. Jesus used stories to teach and to encourage, and to inspire others to live bigger lives. If you were to pick up the Bible, page after page, you'd find nothing but one parable after another.

This past weekend I caught an episode of VH1 Storytellers, where legendary showman, Bruce Springsteen, was the featured artist. I'm not much of a music fan, but this was different. He would sing a verse,

then he would stop, and, for a moment, he would explain the story behind the lyrics. He would then tie the words and the emotions that he was feeling, back to the day he wrote the song. In-depth, he explained what was happening in his life at that time. His feelings, about everything. About his wife and kids. He explained the meaning behind the metaphors and the analogies. He even explained the reasons why he chose those specific ones.

Then he'd sing another verse. Then he'd stop....

Sixty minutes later is was over, and for sixty minutes, I had been sucked into the story *behind* the music.

I didn't care about the music. I cared about the *Story*!

When I think of all the people I've studied in regards to marketing, influence, and creating a movement—from Joel Osteen and Pastor Rick Warren in the religious sector, both of whom operate megachurches with tens of thousands of members, to "radicals" like Glenn Beck, Porter Stansberry and of course, Rush Limbaugh, with hundreds of thousands to millions of listeners and subscribers, to direct-response copywriters like the late Gary Halbert or, Dan Kennedy to whom I've now given money to for seven consecutive years for his advice and entrepreneurial guidance... I have found there is a commonality that unites each of these people, that makes them more *alike* than different. Just like ole Springsteen and Jesus, each is a storyteller. They captivate and fascinate, entertain and sell (...products, services, and even their beliefs) using *story,* and its power, as their weapon of choice.

On that call we also discussed her ambitions. If she could do anything in the world, absent any consideration in regards to business or need to earn income, "What would she want to do?" She said "Speak with kids." To teach kids the important life lessons she's learned, not taught in school. The kinds of lessons that save kids from moving down dark alleys and onto wrong paths. Together we discussed how this could be done. How she could get her message into schools. In front of the principles and teachers and, ultimately, the kids she wishes to impact and inspire.

We also discussed how her ambition could be coupled with her business. We discussed some of the strategies, some of the tactics. But mostly, we discussed the importance of her *story*... how to craft it... how to tell it... and how to get others to buy "into it" so that those that heard it, felt compelled to share it.

I think it's important to understand, if you wish to have a following of any substantial size – for your services, for your message, for your business—mastering the ability to tell influential stories is not optional. It is required.

There is an *Unfortunate Truth* that goes with this fact.

Nothing is more difficult to learn, than to learn how to tell influential stories. Stories, that serve a purpose. Stories, that open peoples' eyes to new possibilities. Stories, that expose flaws in old mindsets. And that offer new and different perspectives.

Nothing, I repeat, nothing is more challenging or difficult, in marketing or advertising, than learning how this is done.

And that's the key point here!

Before you can tell an influential story, and before that story can be *influential*, you have to know what your purpose *is* for telling the story that you're about to tell, in the first place.

When someone reads it, if its about you, or if its about your business, what is the response that you want from the reader? What is the message or takeaway that you want that person to remember and never forget? What are the emotions that you want him to feel and experience? What actions, upon reaching the end of your story, do you want the reader to be motivated to take? Do you want the reader to respond to an advertisement? Maybe you want him to see you differently, more trustworthy or more authoritative?

Or do you want him to do something else, like recruit new clients to your business, for you, because he feels compelled to tell family and friends about the story he just read?

Only by knowing the answers to these questions before you start to tell your story, can you be sure to tell the *right* story.

In the words of Mark Twain, "The difference between the *right* word and the *almost* right word is the difference between lightning and a lightning bug." The same can be said about the *right* story and the *almost* right story— one is just a collection of words on the paper. The other is the power to move mountains and to create a movement; for yourself, or for your business or cause.

When I first met Protector/Social Superhero member, Cheryl Gordon, she said to me, "I don't want to be *just* a real estate agent. I want to be someone who gives back and builds a legacy, something my children and husband can be proud of." And to be clear, Cheryl had been very successful as a real estate agent up to this point. *But...* that's not how she wanted to be defined.

And who can blame her? Who really wants to be seen as a real estate agent, or judged, as a real estate agent is judged?

So we got to work!

We started by repositioning all of her marketing. A process I refer to as *Delinking & Disconnecting,* from all visible symbols, and negative reputations and stereotypes that come as "baggage" to the term "real estate agent."

In short, you can't be different, if you look or sound the same. So Cheryl learned to speak a new language as well.

From there we began to craft her *Character* and the stories that she would need to tell, to position herself as a Protector, Innovator, and Philanthropist—new reputations that would give her power and influence, leaving behind, permanently, any resemblance of her former "real estate agent" label and stereotype.

Following that, within two months she became the founder and CEO of Durham's Teacher Only Program®. She also, with me as her business-partner co-founded an ENG chapter in her marketplace (DurhamENG.com)—establishing herself as a leader in her local business community. And through the application process, using ENG as the vehicle, Cheryl quickly built-up a large referral network of high-level business owners and entrepreneurs. She also became the author of multiple trust and authority articles, reports and even started the process of putting together a book to position her as the *Keeper of Secrets* to prospective clients (Differentiation Strategy #4), titled, "The Warren Buffett Approach to Sell Real Estate: A practical guide to protect yourself from REAL ESTATE

GREED & how to bank an extra $30,000 in profit by taking a VALUE-DRIVEN APPROACH."

Cheryl's customer appreciation event, also, was repositioned to serve a philanthropic purpose; from Outdoor Movie Night, to Outdoor Movie Night *For Hunger*™. And by adding the required elements for *Creating a Movement* to the promotion of her event, she increased the attendance by over 400%. From just a few hundred the previous year, which included family, friends and the neighbors who lived in her neighborhood, to nearly 2,000 people that involved her entire community.

The event itself, was a huge success.

The media, of course, loved it. More than 3,000 lbs. of food was collected for the local food bank. It even attracted as sponsors, globally recognized brands, Mercedes Benz, Lowes, and Sun Life Financial. Not to mention, thirty or so other local businesses and more than 20 community partners, including two school districts and the public library, all of whom provided free promotion.

With the train now rolling down the tracks, the next month, Cheryl doubled down on her philanthropic efforts. Cheryl was on a mission to inspire a movement of giving. She decided to do a *Turkey Drive* for the holidays, and vowed to feed 1500 families in her community.

Promotion, this time was easier.

Using the large database she'd built-up from her previous event, *Outdoor*

Movie Night For Hunger™, Cheryl reached out to these people—told the *right* stories to inspire her readers into action—and within 60 days, raised over $39,000, the equivalent of more than 1500 turkey dinners, and achieved her goal.

And, as Cheryl and her team volunteers, including her parents, husband, and two kids, assembled the meals, the news cameras were there to capture it.

The next month, again, she vowed to give back to her community. This time, she created an event called, *Free Family Skate Night*™, where she rented out the local ice-skating rink and invited the entire community to come skate for free. Again, she became a media darling and again, she made the front-page of her local newspaper.

In the first six months of working with Cheryl, to position her as something more than just a "real estate agent,"—to build a legacy, something she and her family, her husband and kids could be proud of—to her credit, she has made the local newspaper nearly ten times, was talked about on the radio multiple times, even invited to appear on TV to discuss passion and mission to make a difference, during a popular daytime talk show.

In no time flat, by having a message and purpose that drives her, Cheryl has positioned herself as a *Someone*!

"So what is my purpose in life?"

As I stated previously: I believe as a parent, as a friend, as a mentor, as a marketing consultant, as whatever "title" you wish to give me or others assign me—I believe my purpose is to inspire. To lift up and encourage others to dream. To think big. And not just big. But huge. To not be afraid to imagine the impossible. To keep hope alive and not be fearful of the unknown. To not be cowardly in times when courage is needed. To step up when others won't. I believe my purpose is to help others to un-cork and un-bottle, to un-lock the potential locked inside themselves. I believe my purpose is to help others expand their vision to see what is *actually* possible and not just what society tells us is possible. I believe my purpose is to help others create their own destiny and to fulfill their own unique mission.

Cheryl didn't want to *just* be a "real estate agent."

Selling homes and making money is great, but she didn't want her life to amount to "the # of new leads and closed transactions" on a whiteboard in her office. Cheryl wanted to build a legacy that she, her husband and kids, Mother and Father could be proud of.

She is now sought-out by others in her community to give Keynote talks, to be a mentor to other business-owners and

entrepreneurs, to consult on fundraising events, not to mention is no longer seen or judged as a "real estate agent."

She is admired and respected.

Never rejected.

Just this past week, as I am writing this chapter, Cheryl was nominated as an honorary member of Beta Sigma Phi sorority, for her contributions to the community. Below is the short write-up from her monthly newsletter. In the section toward the bottom, third paragraph, you will instantly recognize Differentiation Strategy #2 at play here: Affinity Connection—"a spontaneous or natural liking" between Cheryl and the women of this organization.

SORORITY GIRL?! CHERYL GORDON?!

ΒΣΦ

When I think of Sororities I have flashbacks of teen movies portraying the idea of these perfect blonde college girls who join together in a sisterhood of evil. The leader of the pack is of course the most evil and always ends up losing her boyfriend to the more naturally beautiful girl next door who was against all of the evil practices from the start.

Needless to say when I got a call from local Sorority-Beta Sigma Phi letting me know I was nominated as an honorary member for my contributions to our community, I was a little skeptical! I am happy to report after my first meeting and being introduced to the amazing members... my idea of Sorority couldn't have been more wrong. I couldn't be more humbled and honoured to have been asked to sit as a new honorary member! So thank you Beta Sigma Phi for this honour!

Beta Sigma Phi is an organization of women dedicated to building long lasting friendships with local women in the community, all the while giving back to the local charities they hold dear. Whether it's donating time from their schedules to give a helping hand or providing financial support through their many fundraisers, these women take pride and love being a part of making a difference in their own backyards. Beta Sigma Phi is an opportunity for remarkable women to build a strong circle of friends and enjoy all the enriching benefits of being a part of this beautiful sisterhood.

For more information about visiting a local chapter in your community please contact Nadine Ross:
E-Mail: nross202@rogers.com
Website: www.betasigmaphi.org

Cheryl was also invited to speak to the 200 women that are part of the Beta Sigma Phi organization. Below are her brief comments, recapping how the night went.

| Cheryl Gordon | I did a 15 min speech last to 200 women that are a part of the sorority. Went really well I think. Was bombarded at the end. One woman wanting to sell her house and a few other just wanting to chat. Others wanting to help with some of my initiative. One woman from children's aid wants me to come speak at an event they are having as well. Was pretty neat. All I did was adapt my personal narrative. | 5:31 AM |

At the end of her talk she was bombarded. Some just wanted to chat, to ask her questions. One woman wanted to sell her house. Others wanted to help Cheryl in her various projects, to give back to the community, to make a difference. Another wanted Cheryl to come speak at her event. All in all, not a bad night. She picked up a new client, secured another speaking engagement, met some amazing people and birthed new relationships, increased her status as a *Someone*, she even recruited some new evangelists for her cause.

This is the power of becoming: A *Storyteller.*

I have often said and thought, nothing is more frustrating than being rejected or ignored by those you know you could help. Nothing is more humiliating, than appearing small and insignificant, because you must beg family and friends, and chase people to do business with you. Nothing is more hurtful, than not being able to provide for your family; wife, kids, husband or others that depend on you, because you couldn't secure enough new clients for your services.

For most—proven by the failure rate, 85 to 90% of all new agents—the profession of real estate, is a greener pasture that quickly turns into the "thing" that sucks the life out of them.

One can only take so much rejection.

One can only prospect so much, and do to others what they hate being done to themselves i.e. be contacted by a telemarketer, so many times before they realize that they have *become* the very salesperson that they despise.

When you become a storyteller, though, and learn to tell influential stories for the purpose of strategic positioning. That all changes.

If you were to ask Cheryl how she defines herself, I've never asked her, but I'm certain she would tell you, "I'm a storyteller." Of course, she is much more than that. But, so much of what she has achieved, in such a relatively short period of time—in less than 12 months—is because she is a storyteller.

I too, am a storyteller.

Only through being a *storyteller* and labeling myself as such, am I able to engage people on emotional ground, where they're *susceptible* to being "sucked in" to the message, and reached on a deeper level.

Without the *power of story*, fulfilling my purpose would be impossible.

I believe the same is probably true for you, and yours!

I've come to realize my real purpose in life, and through my P/SS program, is to help others become great storytellers. The best marketers *ARE* the best storytellers.

The people with the largest followings; of clients, subscribers, members or listeners—*ARE* the people who *ARE* the best storytellers. That's what we do here. We learn to tell effective stories. We craft them. We share them. We help each other improve them.

We are *Storytellers*!

And, if that sounds ridiculous to you, you have revealed just how little you know about marketing or influence. Or about creating a *Movement* for your business.

The *right* story can unite or divide a nation.

What makes you think it couldn't position you as a *Someone* in your marketplace, and, as the *Leader* of your own Movement? With the advent of Impact Club®, we have become more effective at this than ever. (See Figure 17-1 through 17-6). One time "real estate agents," now seen as philanthropists and Leaders of a *Movement* in their local community.

To see more visit: www.ImpactClub.com. (An organization committed to Forging Elite Storytellers™. Inspiring the Uninspired. To create a movement of movements by helping others to create their own.)

Relevant Podcast Episodes: 13, 60, 68, 72, 100, 103, 104

Recommended Resources:

• **Protector Videos Series** (Access inside Member Site)

• **Case Study Interviews** (Access inside Member Site)

• **Value-Driven Approach** (www.TheValueDrivenApproach.com)

• **AMS Podcast** (www.AMSpodcast.com)

• **Forging Elite Storytellers** (www.StoryAthlete.com)

• **90-Day Immersion** (www.90DayImmersion.com)

• **Explore ImpactClub®** (www.ImpactClub.com)

EIGHTEEN

The Ultimate Truth:
YOU CAN'T HELP EVERYONE
"Choose Carefully!"

By Ryan Fletcher

Can I confess something to you?

When I founded my company, Agent Marketing Syndicate®, and first started working with real estate agents, I fucking hated it. I thought I would enjoy it, but I quickly realized I hated it.

Every day I felt the life being sucked out of me. More depressing was the thought, that I walked away from, by many people's standards, a "dream job" where I had prestige, respect and power, and was making several hundred-thousand per year and, more than 6-figures in royalties alone, to start this venture. And, lo and behold, I hated it.

It occurred to me, maybe I made a mistake.

You might ask, what was I doing before I founded AMS and I started working with real estate agents? Why did I step down from the position, that, incidentally, many other marketers, copywriters, and entrepreneurs envied me for having?

It's a long story. If you have time, though, I'll tell it to you. Let me take you back. All the way back. To understand why I *hated* working with real estate agents, in this new business that I had founded—the same one that I now love—it would probably help if you knew a thing or two about me. Not on a business-level, but a personal-level.

The year was 2008.

Financially speaking, I had just turned around my real estate business, from making just $8,832 in my first year, to over $180,000 in my second. And, I had just enjoyed another good year. I was 25 years old and making more money than my parents ever had. Up to that point, I had never had more than $5,000 in my bank account. So, this was a big change. I literally thought I was rich, which reveals to you just how naïve and foolish I was when I was 25.

The breakthrough for me, though, that led to this turnaround— which is what you're probably most interested in—was discovering the skill of direct-response copywriting.

A few years before this, back in 2006, I was in my first year in real estate. I was broke. I was also depressed. I'm not going to lie. I never intended to be living the life I am now—as an author, entrepreneur, marketing consultant, etc.

From an early age, I wanted to be a doctor. After shattering my leg in a freak snow-skiing accident when I was 12, and experiencing first hand, the skill and craftsmanship of my orthopedic surgeon, his ability to put my leg back together—something inside of me—I just knew that practicing medicine is what I wanted to do with my life.

From that point forward, becoming a doctor was my sole focus. Sure, I loved sports too, like any kid. But, I always knew that I wanted to find my way into medicine.

This journey led me to volunteer hundreds of hours at the local ER's, job shadow some of the best surgeons in the NW, including the Portland Trailblazer's orthopedic surgeon, Dr. Roberts. I even spent three months on a medical mission in South Africa, where, with a team of doctors and nurses and other pre-med students, we delivered talks on AIDS education and provided treatment for other illnesses.

Below are some of the best smiles you will ever see. Look close, I'm in there.

Everything was going just as I had planned. And, after I graduated from Washington State University, with a near 4.0 GPA in pre-med, I thought for sure I would be accepted to medical school. That first year, I applied to about a dozen different schools. The second year, I applied to another dozen. My third and fourth year of applying, I did the same.

Still no luck.

This led to depression.

Everything I had worked for, I felt like it had been yanked out from underneath me. In a heap of self-pity, I found myself drinking five and six nights a week. During the low-point in my life, I almost lost my fiancé too, but that's a story best told another time. She said eleven words to me that hurt me more than any other words ever said to me. But they also inspired change.

Anyhow, to make ends meet, pay the bills and, to be able to buy Christmas presents for my family, in November of that year, I took a job as a UPS box boy. It was minimum wage job. The checks were small, but at least they were consistent. And they served their purpose, providing me a little extra cash to get by.

December 11th, 2006.

On December 11th, 2006—with what little money I had left from my UPS paycheck, about $19 and some change—I walked into Barnes & Noble to purchase a book for my sister. This would be her Christmas present. Then, on my way to find the book that she wanted, something happened. I don't really believe in fate. I'm not a religious person, I'm not a very spiritual person either, but fate, intervened. I had never taken a business or marketing class in my life. I had no experience in business, and frankly, I wasn't all that interested in marketing. I honestly thought this whole "real estate" thing would just be a year or two gig, until I could get accepted into medical school.

So, to say that I was looking for the book that I ended up finding, would be a lie—it found me.

That book, *The Ultimate Sales Letter* by Dan Kennedy.

For whatever reason, it caught my eye. It was on the shelf, tipped over just so, so that when I walked by, it was the only book cover that I could see. I picked it up and, inside, as I flipped through the pages, it said you could write letters and get clients.

I had never heard of direct-response marketing before. And, I had no clue what the term "copywriting" meant. So both were foreign to me, but I said to myself, "Fuck, that sounds cool. Write letters. Mail letters. Get clients."

I suspended my disbelief, and bought the book.

Since I only had enough money to buy one book, my sister didn't get a gift that year. But I made it up to her the next year.

Long story short, this book changed my life. I know that sounds cliché, and if you own this book, *The Ultimate Sales Letter*, then you know that it's a fairly basic book for *beginning* copywriters and direct-response marketers—nothing too advanced or sophisticated.

But my eyes had been opened.

I have a very addictive personality, and that book provided me my first "taste." I became obsessed.

As an aside, I can't express to you how thankful I am to have found Dan Kennedy. There are a million other authors out there, who have written a million other books. And, to find this one, by Kennedy, a guy that I had never heard of or met, and didn't know anything about until I found his book— has been a godsend.

If you're familiar with Kennedy, you know why I say this. If you're not, I encourage you to become a student of his work. To this day, seven years later, I am still subscribed to his paid newsletter and, a devout student of his teachings.

But it was that first book, from Kennedy, that led to me to

discover the late, legendary ad man, Gary Halbert, who then led me to study many other greats in the fields of marketing, advertising, and, of course, copywriting—the skill that makes effective marketing and advertising possible. Among those studied; David Ogilvy, Victor Schwab, Claude Hopkins, John Caples, Joseph Sugarman, Joseph Crossman, Eugene Schwartz, Robert Collier, to the more contemporary Gary Bencivenga and John Carlton, and many lesser-known names as well, Benjamin Hart Melvin Powers, Lyman P. Wood, and the list continues.

I told you, I have an addictive personality. Once I'm hooked, I become obsessed. It's why I've never tried an illegal drug, my greatest fear is that I would like it.

But I digress. Back to the story. Everything was going great.

After a miserable first year in real estate, I was now making a nice 6-figure income. *But*…there was a problem. I didn't really care about real estate. I wasn't passionate about real estate. It paid the bills, sure. It provided me a certain, very comfortable lifestyle, but it didn't fascinate me.

My mistress was marketing and copywriting. I found myself "cheating" on, and neglecting my real estate business, to study the art and skill of copywriting.

So I made the decision to shut down my real estate business.

I decided I wanted to be a copywriter. At the time, I'm not sure I even knew what that meant, I just knew I wanted to write, tell influential stories, and be *paid* to learn this skill, instead of doing it on the side when I could squeeze it in, or at midnight, after my wife went to bed.

Further, I decided if I was going to do this—I wanted to study with and learn from the best in the world.

At the top of my hit-list, there was a company called Agora, Inc. Dan Kennedy and Gary Halbert often to referred to Agora as a "big time player" in the direct-marketing space. I had also remembered them saying, the best copywriters in the world write for Agora and other large publishers, like Boardroom and Rodale.

It just so happened, when I jumped on their website, again, call it "fate" or "luck"…or just "good timing," whatever, but a division within Agora was looking to hire a junior copywriter. The problem was, well, there were two problems. The first problem, the position only paid a measly $32,000 a year. The second problem, the job was in Delray Beach, Florida.

I lived in Vancouver, Washington—3,000 miles away.

Also, my wife, Melanie, had just been hired on with the Vancouver School District, as a kindergarten teacher. I knew how much that job meant to her. I also knew how hard it was to get hired on, and how hard she had worked.

So I said to her, "It's up to you."

"I want to go. I'd love to go. But if you don't want to go, your family is here, I'll understand."

She asked, "Where did you say it was?"

"Delray Beach. Florida," I said, "It's about 8 miles north of Boca Raton, and about 45 minutes north of Miami."

Then, I'll never forget it. She got a big smile on her face, "Sounds kind of tropical," she said.

"Does that mean you'll go," I asked.

"Yes," she said.

This was in March sometime, on a Tuesday. I don't remember the exact date, I just remember it was a Tuesday because on that following Thursday, is when I sent off my application.

The next two days, I wrote the sales letter and "resume"—that would decide my fate. Thankfully, this was a true direct-response company, so my results and my ability to sell shit were all that mattered. The fact that I didn't have a bachelor's degree in marketing or a large "design" portfolio, to my credit, was not a deterrent.

To apply, I was simply asked to write a sales letter to sell a book or a newsletter, or another subscription-based item.

The letter I wrote, sold Kennedy's *The Ultimate Sales Letter* book—the very book that started me down this path.

As I am writing this, I couldn't find a copy of the sales letter I wrote, but I did find the one-page cover sheet, sent along with the sales letter—shown to the right.

The following Tuesday I got a call from the publisher of the division. They liked what I had written and wanted me to visit Delray Beach for an interview. I booked a ticket, the next week Melanie and I were in Florida.

While I went on my interview, Melanie visited the local school districts. Three days into our trip, both of us were offered jobs—Melanie was now a third grade teacher, and I was a junior copywriter—so we started hunting for apartments. We found a nice townhouse that backed up to a lake. Which is nothing special in

South Florida, everything backs up to a lake. Half the state is underwater.

When we returned home, we broke the news to our parents. My parents thought I was kidding. My mom tried to reason with me. "Can't you do it here? This copywriting thing..." I said to her, "If I'm going to be the best, I have to study with the best." My Dad just cried. For months after I moved, he barely spoke to me. He was angry. He was bitter. He truly thought I would never move back.

Now that I'm a parent myself, I can understand my Mom and Dad's reaction. Every morning I wake up, I can't wait to snuggle with my kids. To not see them, Jackson or Zoey, for weeks, or if they lived across the country, would be devastating. I have told Melanie, "Should we ever end up getting a divorce," which I hope never happens, "just plan on me buying the house next door,  regardless of where you live or with whom, and regardless of how much I have to pay." That's how much my kids mean to me.

Anyhow, after breaking the news to our parents, the following week, I moved to Delray Beach, Florida, while Melanie stayed behind to finish out the school year.

I was almost fired, before I even started.

I'm not shitting you. I moved 3,000 miles across the country, and was almost fired before I started.

Agora, Inc.—something you might not know—most of its divisions sell financial research, in the format of email subscriptions and print newsletters. Well, I didn't know a damn thing about the financial markets. Bull market. Bear market. Maybe naïve, but I didn't know what either meant.

Options. Calls. Spot Market. Trading on margin. Using leverage. My head was spinning, and frankly, my boss began to question if hiring me was a mistake.

I convinced him to give me 30-days to prove to him, that he didn't make a mistake.

Here's the thing: What I don't know but need to know, I will learn. I'll buy books. Go to the library. Contact and interview experts, to pick their brain. Or, in this case, I asked to be pointed in the direction to the sales letters archives. In order to learn what I needed to know, to sell financial shit, I needed access to all the "biggest winners," from all the twenty-plus divisions within Agora, that have ever been written.

The next day, in my email, I found a link to a database, with a user login and password.

This is something, again, I learned from Kennedy. To get really good at copywriting, really fast, you need to study the biggest winners. You need to look for the commonalities. You need to break down each sales letter into its components, and look for the repeated themes and storylines. This trumpets the advice of David Ogilvy, who lamented on the importance of finding the Big Idea. In fact, below are his exact words:

"Big Ideas. Unless your advertising is built on a Big Idea, it will pass like a ship in the night. It takes a Big Idea to jolt the consumer out of his indifference, and take action. Big Ideas are usually simple ideas. Said Charles Kettering, the great General Motors inventor: 'This problem, when solved, will be simple.' Big, simple ideas are not easy to come by. They require genius—and midnight oil."

This is what I was after, in my research binge, as I deconstructed the biggest winners and burned up the "midnight oil"—I was looking for the Big Ideas. I knew if I came up with a Big [Enough] Idea for the sales letter that I needed to write, it would offset my lack of knowledge and understanding of the financial markets.

In other words, I didn't need to know what an option was, I just needed to know how to sell one.

You should have seen the look on people's faces, in the office, when I printed more than 80,000 sheets of paper. I went back over a decade, and printed every "Big Winner" I could find. And yes, in case you're wondering, 80,000 sheets of paper fills a lot of three-ring binders.

A case of paper contains ten reams of 500 sheets each, or 5,000 sheets. So when Office Depot delivered 16 cases of paper to the office, and then, when I ran the printer from morning til night, most didn't quite know what to think.

I told you, I wanted to be the best and I was willing to do anything to achieve it.

I didn't shut down a 6-figure real estate business and move to Florida—3,000 miles away— for a $32,000/year salary, or ask Melanie to quit her job, just to be "okay." I could have been a mediocre copywriter at home.

Here, I had a gold mine at my finger tips. I had a vast archive of the best sales letters that had ever been written—the most valuable resource any *true* marketer or copywriter could ever imagine, and, if they could, would pay a fortune for. So, if they fired me, I wanted to have it all printed off and in hard-copy format. Because you know damn well, as did I, that they weren't going to let me keep my login and password.

So I printed it all.

Then I bought a hundred or so yellow hi-liters, a bunch of red pens, and I got to work. I hi-lited and scribbled notes in the margins, sales letter after sales letter, day after day.

Something I learned from Halbert, a good copywriter will spend 80% of his time researching, and only 20% of his time actually writing. And given the fact that I had a month to produce the sales letter that would determine my fate, I had 24 days to research and 6 days to write.

Looking back, it was a blessing in disguise that Melanie was still back in Vancouver, and couldn't move at the same time I did. Because I worked 18 to 20 hours a day, I didn't have any distractions. From sun up to sun down, and then more each night, I deconstructed sales letters. I had planned to buy a TV, once I got moved in, but never did, out of fear that I would want to watch it— taking time away from my research.

Fear drove me. I didn't want to fail.

I kid you not, I was driven by fear. The idea of being fired and the thought of having to be seen, limping home, as the kid who got "chewed up and spit out" by the big city, terrified me.

I had my doubters. I had my critics. The last thing I wanted to do was prove them right.

At the end of the third week, I started writing, giving myself a few extra days to guarantee completion. I had one shot at this, all my eggs were in one basket.

Using the research I had collected, I mapped out the sales pitch. I had been debating between 3 different Big Ideas, and didn't know which one to choose. Do you know how I decided? I flipped a coin. I thought they were all good, I just couldn't choose. Plus, about that time, the second movie in the latest Batman trilogy had just came out, *The Dark Knight,* and I noticed to make decisions, Harvey Dent, would just flip a coin.

Heads or tails would determine my fate.

So I grabbed a quarter, and flipped it twice. I created two head-to-head match ups between the Big Ideas, and chose to live with the outcome. With three days to spare, I finished writing that sales letter. Over the next few days, I read it again and again, making small edits.

That next Monday, after the weekend, I took it to my boss. His reaction, wasn't good. I don't remember the exact words, but I definitely remember how the flow of the conversation went.

"WTF? This is it?" he said, "I give you 30 days to prove yourself. And this is it? This is what you bring me? This piece of shit?"

I was dumbfounded. I didn't know what to say, or what to think. I didn't know how to respond.

All I remember saying is, "Just test it."

"Please! Just test it."

I just remember pleading my case.

I moved 3,000 miles. I signed a 12-month lease. I put my heart and soul into this bitch.

"Please, just test it," I said, "If it doesn't work. You won't even have to fire me. I'll quit. I'll pack up my office. I'll quit."

"You'll have the satisfaction of knowing you were right. I was wrong."

"Please just test it."

Thankfully, he agreed.

Later that night, I was speaking to Melanie on the phone. She asked, "How's it going?"

I didn't really know how to answer.

I said, "I guess it all comes down to next week's test. Either I'm going to get promoted or fired."

Half-joking but not really, she said "Well let me know which before I move 3,000 miles."

The campaign I wrote was unlike anything they had ever done before. So it was either going to work, or it was going to bomb. At least, that's what I believed in my mind. I suppose, in truth, there could've been a hundred different variations of success or failure, like shades of grey, but I envisioned the all or nothing outcome.

The previous best sales letter that any copywriter had ever written for this particular division of Agora, was just a tick over one-million dollars.

On the day of the test, as I awaited the results, it was the first time I had ever felt like time stood still. Every minute felt like an hour. And, the way that the reporting system worked, sales updates only came out at 7:00am, 11:00am and 4:00pm. So while I only had to wait about 4 hours between updates, the wait was painstaking.

By the end of day one, I knew my fate. And, so did everyone else.

That sales letter is still being talked about, five years later.

I have a good friend that works as a copywriter for the largest division of Agora, called S&A Research. In an email he sent me just this past month, as of this writing, he said, "Funny—your name keeps coming up here every so often. We still study your 'beta-tester' sales letter."

In its first week, that "piece of shit" sales letter, as my boss called it, generated more than a million dollars in sales, breaking the previous record for my division. At its peak, it generated a million dollars in new sales per day. And, over the next six months, it sold more than $15-million worth of services.

On the next page is the email sent to me and throughout the division, when we passed the $10-million mark.

You'll notice the increased sales volume, when it came time to calculate my royalties, presented the accounting department with a "new" problem that they had not ever faced.

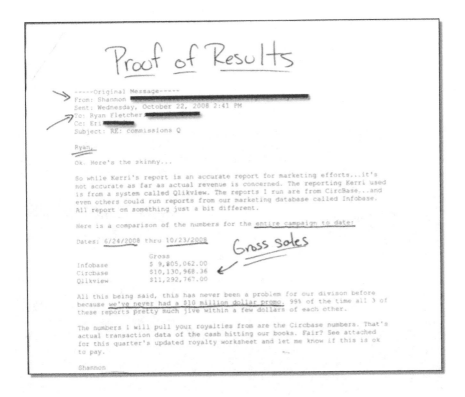

Long story short, I didn't get fired. I didn't have to pack up my office or have to quit. In fact, I was promoted. The next five sales letter I wrote, all did over a million dollars in sales.

Within 18-months of arriving at Agora, I went from Junior Copywriter to Senior Copywriter, and then, became the CMO: Chief Marketing Officer of the division, replacing the guy who hired me.

The sweetest revenge!

I was just 27 years old and, I was a marketing executive for a $25-million division of Agora, Inc. One of the largest players in the world of direct-response marketing. *I had made it.*

Life was good. The money was great. I lived a life that most have only ever dreamed of. I was constantly being chauffeured, from one all-expense paid trip to the next. Paris. Bermuda. Panama. I even spent a week in a Chateau, in the French countryside, with a small group of the best copywriters in the world, from all the divisions. For five days, from sun up to sun down, we exchanged secrets and techniques. You couldn't have asked for a greater learning experience.

To make $5,000 to $8,000 in a day was nothing.

I worked by day and drank by night. Why all CEOs drink Scotch (neat) I have no clue. I never acquired a taste for it.

And, to think, just 18-months earlier, I was just a "real estate agent."

When I went to Agora I wanted—simply—to be *the* best.

Today, I'm often asked, "How did you do it?"

Or questions like, "What's your secret?"

Of course, the real question being asked is, "Why are you so much more successful than me?" or "How did you become so much more successful than me?"

My answer is always the same. "I have more binders than you." As you can imagine, this response always confuses them. "What?" they ask, "More binders?"

"Yes" I say, "More binders."

I didn't print off 80,000 pages of the best sales letters ever written for my health—I did it because I wanted to learn.

You don't become the best by learning one or two cheap secrets, nor do you go from being a *no one* to being a *Someone* in 18-months—and still be talked about today, five years after having walked away from the tallest mountains of direct-response—by only being casually interested in marketing and advertising.

You have to be obsessed.

You have to be willing to print 80,000 pages of the best sales letters ever written, and be willing to deconstruct sales letter after sales letter so that, when those *Big Ideas* reveal themselves, you can spot the repeated themes and storylines.

A sales letter is, literally, nothing more than an influential story, that makes the case, for your ability to produce superior results for your clients.

"What's that?"

"But you don't have access to that database, that I did?"

It's true, most people, probably, including you, will never have access to the Agora archives. But there are other ways to learn and master the skill of copywriting. There are, also, other ways you can learn to tell influential stories. For starters, you could start by studying any businessperson or public personality, that enjoys a large following; of members, subscribers, readers, listeners, clientele—any audience of substantial size. After all, the purpose of a sales letter is to build the size of your audience.

Most business owners and entrepreneurs don't understand this, including most real estate agents. They hear the phrase "$15 million in sales" and think, "This doesn't apply to me or my business. I don't have a product to sell." And, if that's what you're thinking, let me stop you there. Because it's a stupid thought. *You* are the product. Your product is yourself, your knowledge and expertise, and hopefully—Differentiation Strategy #4—your unique approach.

How you choose to package that product, through the stories you tell, determines your level of success or failure. *Besides.* What that "$15-million sales" represents, really, is a large number of new clients—thousands and thousands—who were attracted to this one man's services because of the message in a 22-page letter.

It is not just money in the bank. It represents *real* people. *New clients!*

And, isn't that what you want, a large NEW audience of prospects and clients?

So, for starters, you could study people in the public marketplace—just as I have done—that have created a "movement" for their business, idea or cause.

And, as much as it pains me to say this, you could start with the President of the United States, Barack Obama.

You could print off the over 400 emails that Obama and his team sent out, during his record-breaking campaign, that produced more than 10-million individual donors. You could break down each email into categories, analyze each email for their commonalities, separate the tactics from the strategies, and make a detailed list of all repeated themes and storylines.

This would be a good place to start. Especially since, politicians and real estate agents, aren't that far separated in terms of negative stereotype and reputation. Nobody trusts either of them.

Further, you could research in-depth, religious leaders who have massive followings. People like Pastor Rick Warren or the more prominent and visible, Joel Osteen.

Osteen is the pastor of Lakewood Church in Houston. America's largest and fastest growing church. A church so large, his Sunday service takes place in a former sports arena. Over 40,000 people pack the former Compaq Center on a weekly basis, to hear Joel's message, not to mention the 7 million more he reaches each Sunday via television broadcast.

After discovering Dan Kennedy, and learning his philosophy about the power of the "Herd" and "building a Herd", it became my obsession to study people who enjoy a massive following.

I found it fascinating, how these people, like Joel Osteen, could attract 40,000 people a week to his church, when other pastors, like my friend's dad, could barely fill a few pews each Sunday.

And see, you don't need access to a secret database of the best sales letters ever written. Don't get me wrong, it helps. But, you could just buy these people's books and, use them as study devices to deconstruct everything about these people. You could break down their message, piece-by-piece, identify and analyze the commonalities, separate the tactics from the strategies, and, again, make a detailed list of all repeated themes and storylines.

This (too) would be an excellent place to start.

Further yet, you could analyze people like Glenn Beck who has attracted millions of listeners to his talk radio show, The Glenn Beck Program. You could analyze people like Rush Limbaugh, and people like Howard Stern. You could buy several of Beck's books; maybe, *Control: Exposing the Truth About Guns*, and his previous best-seller, *Cowards: What Politicians, Radicals, and the Media Refuse to Say*. Limbaugh's books are also readily available, *See, I Told You So*, and *The Way Things Ought To Be*. Each can be purchased on Amazon and shipped to you for less than $15 bucks.

You could also tune-in to hundreds of hours of GBTV: Glenn Beck TV that boasts over 300,000 paid subscribers and helped Beck a cool
$80 million in 2013. And, just as we did with Joel Osteen, you could begin to deconstruct the intricacies of how he, and others like him, have built their following.

The appropriate term here: *Reverse Engineering*.

What got 'em? What keeps 'em? What compels 'em to recruit others?

This is exactly how I taught myself to the skill of copywriting, in the process, learned to tell influential stories.

I obtained large collections of sales letters, ads, video and webinar scripts, stage presentations, I watched hundreds of hours of infomercials, listened to talk radio non-stop, then broke each message down into its components, deconstructed each pitch, each format, and asked questions while I looked for the commonalities. I separated the tactics from strategies, and categorized everything, as I made a detailed checklist of all repeated themes and storylines.

If you walked into my office, as a consulting client or private client, you'd see twenty-feet of 12-foot high book shelves filled with nothing but 4-inch three-ring binders, and hundreds of books with dogged-eared corners and scribbled-in margins—filled with these blueprints.

You could even dig deeper, by studying regular business people like Mike Dillard, founder of TheElevationGroup.com, who grew his business from zero members to over 40,000 members in just two years. Or people like Porter Stansberry, founder of StansberryResearch.com, a publisher of financial research—also, the largest division of Agora—who, in just over a decade, has gone from zero subscribers to nearly 1,000,000 paid subscribers.

And, again, you could ask: "What got 'em?"..."What keeps 'em?" "What compels 'em to recruit others?"

You could also become a serious student of the comic book industry.

Isn't it interesting that virtually every major blockbuster movie of the past decade is of comic book origins? Spiderman 1, 2, 3, Batman Begins, The Dark Knight, The Dark Knight Rises, Iron Man 1, 2, 3, The Hulk, Captain America 1, 2, Transformers 1, 2, 3, Wolverine 1, 2, X-Men, The Avengers, soon out, Avengers 2, Man of Steel... and the list will continue.

Isn't it fascinating that everyone from small kids to grown men, are obsessed fans of these fictional characters that are *built* entirely "from scratch"?

I think it is. The people getting rich from these characters, also, think it is. So, here are some smart questions I would ask: Why are these characters so addictive? What makes them addictive? How can I infuse myself; my own business and personality, my message and purpose, with that same kind of addiction?

To learn how, for starters, you could read the following books: Batman and Philosophy, X-Men and Philosophy, Spiderman and Philosophy, Iron Man and Philosophy, The Avengers and Philosophy, Green Lantern and Philosophy, Superman and Philosophy; you could also read; Batman and Psychology, The Psychology of Superheroes, Batman Unauthorized, God on the Streets of Gotham. You could also read SuperGods, Supervillains and Philosophy, The Science of Supervillains, The Supervillain Handbook, and, an absolute must, the *New York Times* best-seller,

Marvel Comics: The Untold Story—documenting the epic rise of Marvel, from the brink of failure to becoming a giant, as it was guided by Stan Lee.

You could also call up *Twomorrows Publishing* or visit their website, and purchase all the back issues—as Dan Kennedy advised me to do, on a recent consulting call, as he did for a project pertaining to "Superhero Based Marketing"—of Alter Ego Magazine. This is a fanzine edited by Roy Thomas that breaks down, and dissects the comic book industry. Including, the stories behind the stories, and the stories behind the characters, as the characters were being imagined and built, by their respective writers.

You could also read books on "how to write comics" like, *The DC Guide to Writing Comics*, authored by Dennis O'Neil, as way to master the different aspects of storytelling.

For example, the most important character in any storyline is the villain, or in literary terms, the antagonist. Legendary comic book writer, and largely accepted as the ambassador of the comic industry, Stan Lee, puts it this way, "Sure, you always need a hero, but ask yourself this: How eager would you be to read about a superhero who fought litterbugs, jay-walkers, or income tax evaders?"

What would a good guy be without a bad guy?

This is something everyone from God (and Satan) to Batman (and the Joker) to Disney's Little Mermaid (and Ursula), to the top-ranked news media outlets (Fox News vs. all the liberals), and to the world's best-selling authors have all figured out. Without a bad guy the good guy is fucking boring, and further, who needs a good guy if there isn't bad guy for him to do battle against?

Stories need conflict and resolution: Villains *and* heroes! It is extremely difficult to have a hero, if there is no villain.

James Patterson—the world's bestselling author—who has sold over 300 million copies of his books, and holds the Guinness record for the most #1 *New York Times* bestsellers of any author, has been quoted, "The villains, who tend to drive the plots, must be *at least* as interesting and believable as the heroes, if not significantly more so."

This is why the subtitle of the book that I co-author and license to members of my Protector/Social Superhero program starts with the phrase: A practical guide to protect yourself from REAL ESTATE GREED..." because before we can step in and "save the day" for our clients, first, we must battle the "villains."

In the *Protector Video Series* mentioned at the back of this book, I talk more about this concept. Specifically, in video No. 2 titled, "Why the demand for Protectors is greater than ever, and why, *YOU* are needed."

You could (even) go one step further.

You could read books like, *The True Believer* by Eric Hoffer—an in-depth look at people like Hitler and, on the thoughts and nature of mass movements—both good and evil, but specifically, what drives their creation, propagation, and ultimately destruction. Frankly, I think you'd be surprised by how many great charitable organizations have been built using the blueprint revealed in this book.

Then, taking what you've learned—the psychology of human behavior, the structure and elements of mass movements, and the ability to tell influential stories—you could begin to apply it to your real estate business.

Those Big Ideas that you discovered, along with the repeated themes and storylines that you documented, could serve as the foundation of all your marketing. All your ads. All your sales letters. You could even write a book, built on one of these Big Ideas, that details and explains how your unique approach gets superior results for your clients.

This is how you go from being a no one to being a *Someone* in your industry, inside of 12 months.

And, if you haven't guessed, this is why I hated working with real estate agents when I first founded my company, Agent Marketing Syndicate®, back in 2010. Because every agent I spoke to wanted to be a *Someone*, but when it came down to doing the actual work, and learning the actual skills, everyone had an excuse as to why *they* couldn't do it or, *why* it couldn't be done.

Do you know how hard it is to help someone, who isn't all that keen on helping himself?

Do you know how frustrating it is?

In retrospect, I was to blame. My marketing at the time, attracted entirely the wrong type of person. I didn't do a good job of making it clear, just how difficult the task is, to become a *Someone*.

As a result, I attracted the "all talk, big dreams, but-I-don't-want-to-work too-hard" real estate agent. In the direct-response world, we refer to these scabs as the "opportunity" seekers. They happen to be the worst kind of customer. The kind of folks, I absolutely can't stand—who do nothing but bitch, whine and complain, about just how hard they're working, but never accomplish anything.

So when I redid my marketing—The Protector Video Series, again, there is a link at the end of this book, where you can access these videos—I made sure to make it clear to people, just how difficult and challenging my Protector/Social Superhero program really is, and what would be expected of them, if accepted.

I shared the story about, Sir Earnest Shackleton—a British sailor—and about the advertisement he wrote to recruit adventurers for his voyage to explore Antarctica.

The year was 1913, and on December 29th of that year, Sir Earnest Shackleton ran ad in the London Times that announced a new expedition, a journey to Antarctica to explore the South Pole. The ad itself, was just 26 words long, but quite possibly, the greatest 26 word ad that's ever been written.

Here's what it said, the actual ad as it appeared:

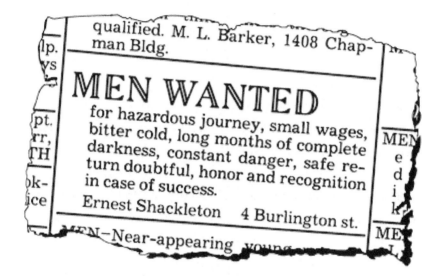

When someone reads this ad, they can't help but to *feel* something inside them. What was your response to it?

Did it cause you to recoil in fear, maybe you said to yourself, "Screw that!" Or, did it give you a little shot of adrenaline?

Depending on how you responded, I can instantly tell whether or not you, or anyone, will be successful within the Protector/Social Superhero program.

And see, this selection—and why it was important—is because Earnest Shackleton was sailing to Antarctica. There was no quitting or getting off the ship. Once you were accepted and once the ship left port, that was it. You were on. There was no turning back. And to survive the journey, everyone needed to do their part. There could be no weak-links or little mush-cookies.

This is why Shackleton's ad was so brilliant, it called out, only to those men who were of the *toughest* mindset.

Within weeks of posting this ad, more than 5,000 men applied to join Shackleton on his expedition. From those, just 27 were chosen. The commonality they all shared, was the willingness to subject themselves to extreme conditions. A punishing journey, just for the possibility to achieve breakthroughs and greatness.

There was no guarantee of success, but these men had more than just balls bigger than you or I. They had courage, and they saw this, as their chance to make their mark.

This too, is why I uprooted my entire life, shut down my real estate business, and moved 3,000 miles away, to Florida, to study with and learn from the best copywriters in the world. Because I saw it, as my chance to make my mark. I didn't want to just be a "real estate agent," any more than Cheryl Gordon did—I wanted to be a *Someone.* I too, wanted to create a legacy, that one day, my family and I, my wife and kids could be proud of. And whatever it took to make that happen, I was willing.

This is why, incidentally, I now love my business and working the agent-members in my P/SS program. Because I no longer waste even a second of my time or energy on those "real estate agents" who aren't just as committed to living out their life's purpose and mission as I was, and still am.

On the following pages, you'll find a few comments from the agent-entrepreneurs that have experienced "what it's like" to be accepted as a member into the Protector/ Social Superhero program.

I like to say we're a tight-knit community of outcasts, broken toys, entrepreneurs, dreamers—but mostly, we're just storytellers—and, just maybe, you'd fit right in.

Which brings me to my main point of this chapter—who you choose to accept as a client in your real estate business, choose carefully. You can't help everyone. Some people are content with being mediocre and getting mediocre results. And trying to help everyone will drain you of all your optimism. Suck the life out of your body, and cause you to hate your business.

So, choose carefully!

My advice, "Never Talk To Anyone, Until They Know You Are A Someone®"—that starts with your ability to tell *influential* stories about yourself, your business, and about your clients.

But first, before you can do that, in my experience, you must embrace the title of *storyteller*.

And see yourself as such.

I want to thank you, sincerely, for reading this book. I have enjoyed this journey with you, and I hope you have too.

If this is your first introduction to me, and my beliefs, my way of thinking about business and marketing—about living your life's mission and purpose; about becoming a *Someone*—then I hope I have a made a good first impression.

Above all, I hope that I have ignited your imagination of what's *really* possible for you, your business, when you allow yourself to embrace your vision, and refuse to be brainwashed by the trainers, coaches and gurus—*The Guru Party*—who control this industry.

There is a better way. It's been presented in this book.

-Ryan Fletcher

I'd love to hear your thoughts and feedback. I do my very best to respond to each person, personally, in a reasonable timeframe. Ryan@AgentMarketingSyndicate.com

Relevant Podcast Episodes: 15, 28, 40, 50, 59, 66, 99, 101, 102

<u>Recommended Resources:</u>

• **Protector Videos Series** (Access inside Member Site)

• **Case Study Interviews** (Access inside Member Site)

• **AMS Podcast** (www.AMSpodcast.com)

• **Value-Driven Approach** (www.TheValueDrivenApproach.com)

• **Forging Elite Storytellers** (www.StoryAthlete.com)

• **90-Day Immersion** (www.90DayImmersion.com)

• **Explore ImpactClub®** (www.ImpactClub.com)

A FEW WORDS

FROM MEMBERS OF THE
(ORIGINAL) PROGRAM

WHO WANTED TO BE

SOMETHING

MORE

THAN JUST

"REAL ESTATE AGENTS!"

Words from Ryan Sloper

Hey man... just wanted to take a second to say THANKS for all that you do!!! I can honestly say that you are one of the people that I am most thankful for this year...

One of the main reasons my business has grown so much over the last year is because I have focused so much on being even more of an authority, staying consistent with my marketing, stepping out of my comfort zone to do video (hard to believe considering I did Live radio for 2 years but video is a different animal...LOL), creating marketing messages/sales letters using stories then getting people to respond with the use of great calls to actions, improving my website by making simple tweaks..... All this has happened because I have bought into YOU and your teachings, and I honestly couldn't be more thankful to have you as a Mentor!!

Before finding you I did study direct-marketing concepts ala Dan Kennedy, Joe Polish, Dean Jackson etc, but you were the first person to be able to break things down on a level that not only could I understand them but I gained the confidence I needed to go out there and IMPLEMENT.

I look forward to another year of IMPLEMENTING. By the way, that quote you said the other day on the call "Vision without execution is delusion" is embedded in my head and I repeat that to myself every morning at least 10 times before I start my day!

Talk soon brother!

FYI... just got done reading the monthly newsletter. Good stuff man! Funny thing is a lot of what you write about are the same conversations going on in my head. I watched "The Profit" all of season 1 and 2 and was saying the same thing...great that you brought in 4 million in revenue but you're not making any money.

The reality is this is the TRUTH for most small businesses, and there is a HUGE opportunity to help them get on the right Track. Hmmm... the Book itself is a walking, breathing marketing piece to get small businesses to reach out for consulting services especially when utilized through ENG :)

Oh...and what you want for ALL of US..."To BE Financially Secure!! "

Please know that there is not a day that goes by that I am not grateful for having come in contact with you, and I truly APPRECIATE all that you DO. There are plenty of people out there that would say something like that and it wouldn't mean shit...but it really is hard to find GOOD people that truly do care about seeing others succeed. You definitely are in that 1% club!

I would actually be more worried about my Financial Success if you refused to take my Money :) Thx again brother!

- Ryan Sloper

Recommended Resources:

- **Protector Videos Series** (Access inside Member Site)

- **Case Study Interviews** (Access inside Member Site)

- **AMS Podcast** (www.AMSpodcast.com)

- **Value-Driven Approach** (www.TheValueDrivenApproach.com)

- **Forging Elite Storytellers** (www.StoryAthlete.com)

- **90-Day Immersion** (www.90DayImmersion.com)

- **Explore ImpactClub®** (www.ImpactClub.com)

Words from Eric Verdi

Flashback to Salisbury State University. Circa 1997.

I remember it like it was yesterday, standing in front of a class of 30 or 40 students-trying my hardest to just regurgitate what I had learned the past four years. My hands were shaking, and I was sweating so bad there were stains on my armpits. I was just staring at the words in front of me, trying to remember what to say next. Was I saying it right? Was I relaying all the information I had spent so much time memorizing?

This is the opposite of a positive storytelling experience. And it is the exact opposite of how our ancestors captured the attention of their audiences. If I had tried this back in the cavemen days, I would have been bonked on the head with a stick.

I was not telling a story that captivated and connected with my audience. I was not winning the trust of my tribe.

You know how the saying goes, back in the days of the caveman, before the written word, stories would be passed down from generation to generation (we wrote about this in our book, "The Psychological Approach to Real Estate"). You see, back then, human beings had no choice but to craft clever tales of adventure, prowess and victory to hold the attention of the group. They couldn't meander on about what they knew or what they had to offer. They had to engage. They had to connect. This is how modern civilization was born.

Today, the same dynamic is true. Except now storytelling skills don't win you the loyalty and respect of your fellow cavemen – they win business. They win you profits, and they win you the life you've always wanted to live – a life you can be proud of.

That day at Salisbury, I realized something very powerful about the spoken world. I realized that what I was afraid was not public speaking at all. I realized I was afraid of not memorizing all of my lines, not saying the words in the right order or not demonstrating everything I had learned through years of research.

I realized I wasn't speaking from the heart. I was regurgitating facts, lines on a page.

Fast forward to now, 2017, and I have a much greater grasp of the power of public speaking and the power of story. Just like with any profession, business or way of life, in real estate you are taught there is a set way of doing things. You are taught to memorize scripts, answer questions and approach objects from potential clients (or even spouses) in a certain way and with a certain tone in order to achieve a set result you are told you should achieve.

In my fifteen years in real estate, I achieved success following this set formula for real estate. I was happy. I was secure, and I had a lot to be thankful for. Yet, somehow something was missing. I wanted bigger and better.

Then, in 2011, I met Ryan Fletcher. I can't remember whether it was a mail piece or a Facebook post that initially drew us together. But as I soon as I met him, his story resonated with me. I had been researching Dan Kennedy at the time, and I could tell Fletcher was a student of his – his writing had all the markings of Dan's client-centered approach to storytelling (If you haven't heard of Dan Kennedy, yet, I suggest you pick up a copy of his book, "The Ultimate Sales Letter." It is the ultimate foundation in writing to win your audience's trust and respect).

Fletcher and I had already learned the amazing power of storytelling from Dan and how to win over your prospect by speaking their language and telling them a story they could understand, relate to and connect with.

We were ready to move on to the next stage of storytelling. We both were hungry for more.

So that's what we did. Since 2011, both he and I have evolved, along with other members of our group. For us, it's no longer about designing the perfect ad or targeting the right niche. It's not about selling a product or a service. It's about who can tell the most compelling story and (like the top dog caveman of the Paleolithic era) build up their tribe. It's about creating a movement.

For the last 5 years, the power of storytelling has completely transformed my life, personally and professionally. Professionally, the business has skyrocketed. There are no cold calls, no chasing, no pestering, no sequential drip campaigns. In fact, we don't sell at all. We create content and tell stories.

What we have done is position ourselves, through the stories we have told (in newsletters, podcasts and magazines) to have a steady stream of natural inbound referrals coming our way every day. Since about 90% of our business comes from past clients or are direct referrals from our current audience these new clients already know our story, how we operate a different model, how we never 'sell.'

And in the rare instance that someone comes to us who has not heard our story, the first thing we do when we meet them is find out theirs. We want to know what makes them tick, what motivates them and what gets them out of bed in the morning. Why? Because when we get them to open up about their fears, wishes and dreams, we open up the most powerful part of themselves and create a perfect foundation on which to connect. Then, we simply share our story with them. We share what makes us different from every other Tom, Dick or Harry down the street.

We listen and truly connect on another level. They become our people, our tribe.

That's why, when we meet with somebody new, we share our story and we want to hear theirs. We might share a story about a client or friend who had a lot of success in real estate (like the couple who followed our game plan to a T, invested in their home and the process, then we scientifically staged their home and they ended up getting an additional $34,000 than their next-door neighbor), and we might share a pitfall to avoid (like a woman who wouldn't budge on her wallpaper and her house sat on the market for 4 months and had to have 3 price reductions to overcome the wallpaper). But we do this through telling stories and through relating other points of reference to our clients.

Thanks to the art of storytelling, our company is seeing an unprecedented level of growth.

Storytelling is also how Frederick Advice Givers was born. It started with a quick conversation I had with Fletcher in 2014. Someone had just come to my office wanting me to advertise in a magazine when the lightbulb went off and I had an *Aha* moment.

I said to Ryan, "Hey Fletch, I want to help other business owners. I want to help other local people share their stories. I want to write for them. I want to help them." I still remember Fletcher's uncanny response. He said "Verdi, Verdi. I love your heart and love what you want to do. But that's too much f**ng work."

He was right, by the way. It was too much work. But here's what he suggested we do instead (which were pretty much doing to a 'T' right now). He said, "Here's what you're going to do. You're going to start a podcast and interview local business owners and entrepreneurs. From there, you will have stories written about them for them to use for their audiences."

So, we did just that.

It took about a year to build out, but by March 2015, we launched Frederick Advice Givers® and have recorded over 100 episodes with local entrepreneurs. In under two years, we have helped over 100 Frederick business owners share their stories. More than that, we have helped these business owners connect with their clients and potential clients.

We used the power of story to build up their tribe. We never sell. We always tell stories. We always connect. Just a word of caution though: you have to really commit. Once you commit to telling stories, the more personal they can become.

And the more personal they become, the tougher they can be to tell. It can be difficult to open up and talk about struggles you have hand, family members who have passed away or tragic events that have happened to you or to people you really care about. But that is real life. That is what people want to hear.

When you open up about these tough times and the lessons they have brought about in your life, people will open up to you. Quid pro quo. When you are open, compassionate and caring in your stories, people will be open, compassionate and caring in their stories to you. People thrive on connections, and they are motivated by common bonds. Storytelling creates bonds. No, more than that, it is the only thing that does.

Recently, we started the Impact Club®, here in Frederick. It's a movement created and supported by Impact Venture Capitalist (our local members) to support local charities in a more powerful way than any one person can do alone.

As co-founder of the Impact Club®, I had to get in front of a group of 200 or 300 people (instead of a small class of 30 or 40) and I had to introduce the concept of the club. I had to get people to understand what it was all about. This there was no script. There was no research. I just got up there and spoke from the heart. I told a story. This time, unlike the 20-year-old Eric Verdi, the 41-year-old Eric Verdi had very little fear of standing up in front of the crowd. I wasn't nervous at all, and I knew in my heart what I wanted to say about the Impact Club®. I knew I wanted to share a story about the Impact Club® and how what we do will affect so many within our community. I wanted to share how, through the club, each person has a direct impact on another human being's life. I wanted to share how we take those small donations and turn them into massive impact.

This time, because I spoke from the heart and told a story, I was able to connect. I was able to inspire and build a club I could be proud of with over 240 members. I was able to put those cavemen storytellers to shame. That is the power of storytelling. It helps create connections between you and your audience and helps to position you in the light that you want to be positioned.

If I can leave you with one parting thought. If you can learn the art of Storytelling, then share this gift with your children it will take them wherever they want to go in life.

- Eric Verdi

(Listen to Eric's Interview on Podcast, between Ep 58 and 59)

<u>Recommended Resources:</u>

• **Protector Videos Series** (Access inside Member Site)

• **Case Study Interviews** (Access inside Member Site)

- **AMS Podcast** (www.AMSpodcast.com)

- **Value-Driven Approach** (www.TheValueDrivenApproach.com)

- **Forging Elite Storytellers** (www.StoryAthlete.com)

- **90-Day Immersion** (www.90DayImmersion.com)

- **Explore ImpactClub®** (www.ImpactClub.com)

Words from Travis Crow

The most empowering decision I've ever made for myself, also turned out to be one of my biggest regrets…. In January of 2016, I was stuck. My real estate business was doing ok, but it wasn't even close to where I wanted it to be. Honestly… I was struggling… Bad… Not just financially, but struggling emotionally as well. I was being told that the only way to succeed in real estate was to cold-call and hound my friends for business.

Doing this made my stomach ache.

I wondered, "Is this the only way to succeed in this business?" There had to be a better way. I wondered after only being in the business for 2 years if I would even be able to keep doing it… The feeling I got when begging for business was sucking the life out of me.

Shortly after that moment, I "stumbled" across a Facebook ad by Ryan Fletcher. I clicked to the website and watched the video. The decision to watch that video would change my life forever…. I joined Ryan's program in March of 2016. My first few weeks in the program were overwhelming. There was just so much information. My first thought was, "Shit, I have to learn to write stories". Over the next 3 weeks, I read every page of material available to me in the program. I dove in and consumed everything I could. It was so engaging that I usually stayed up until well past 1am. I bought book after book, and fell in love with story. (I'm pretty sure as of today I've put one of Amazon's kids through college).

My first few stories were terrible. I questioned everything I wrote. I struggled with thoughts like "No one is going to give a shit about my personal stories".

I was wrong… As my writing got better, my business improved. And the funny thing is, the less I talked about my business, the more business came my way. The more personal I made my stories, the more response I got from my readers. It turns out that, the more you reveal about yourself, like your triumphs and tragedies, the more people connect with you. They crave to hear more and more.

My first year in real estate I sold a total of $2,000,000 worth of homes. Fast forward to January of 2017 and I sold over $2,000,000 worth of homes… In ONE MONTH… All because I took a chance and became a storyteller.

But honestly, the money isn't the best part. I've grown so much as a person. I no longer have limiting beliefs about myself or my abilities. Learning this one craft has made me a better person in every aspect of my life. A confidence in myself that I've never had before. I've realized that, with my new knowledge on crafting stories, I can create anything I want. The power to create and reshape my future is (literally) in my hand. But be careful… Learning to tell a story that connects with people is like getting handed the keys to the greatest super-power in the world. You'll never read a book, watch a movie, or listen to a conversation the same way again. Once the veil is lifted, and you know how to craft a story with a purpose… You can never "unlearn" it.

So that "big regret" that I have?

It's that no one was around to teach me this when I was young. But I get to make up for it. I get to start teaching my 10 year old son about the importance of becoming a great storyteller. That if he masters this skill, he'll have the ability to control his own future and destiny. The world will be his to mold and change in positive ways.

I can't think of a greater gift you could give your child...

(Listen to Travis's Interview on Podcast, between Ep 96 and 97)

<u>Recommended Resources:</u>

• **Protector Videos Series** (Access inside Member Site)

• **Case Study Interviews** (Access inside Member Site)

• **AMS Podcast** (www.AMSpodcast.com)

• **Value-Driven Approach** (www.TheValueDrivenApproach.com)

• **Forging Elite Storytellers** (www.StoryAthlete.com)

• **90-Day Immersion** (www.90DayImmersion.com)

• **Explore ImpactClub®** (www.ImpactClub.com)

Words from Kevin Evers

The true power of a story revealed itself when I least expected it.

Back in 2015, my wife and I went through some tough times. We learned that our first son had a birth defect. Initially, they thought it was something that could be treated after he was born.

That all changed on July 29th, 2015, when a doctor told us three words, "Incompatible With Life." Our son, Noah, would not survive birth.

My hopes and dreams were shattered in an instant. A lifetime of firsts that I would never get to experience. His first words. His first steps. His first day of kindergarten. Playing catch in the backyard. Our first beer.

Our first day together was also going to be our last. I struggled to cope with the roller coaster of emotions. On the surface, I played it tough. Deep down inside though, I was hurting.

We were three months from Noah's due date. We decided to continue with the pregnancy and give him every chance we could. It would take a miracle, but we refused to give up hope.

During those three months, the three of us did everything together. Sporting events, festivals, just about everything you can imagine in a Wisconsin summer, we did it. The memories we made together were amazing. At the end of each day though, reality slowly crept back in.

Family and friends urged me to talk to someone. There was no shortage of recommendations for psychologists that I could meet with. I wasn't crazy. I just wanted to be left alone. I didn't need to talk to anyone. Or so I thought.

My emotions festered deep inside. I would feel "fine" for a number of days, and then out of nowhere, everything would boil over. I quickly grew tired of explaining exactly what was happening every time I ran into someone. It wasn't an easy thing to talk about once, so you can imagine the agony of taking about it dozens of times over. I decided to start writing about it. One morning, I went to the local coffee shop. I got myself a tall cup of black coffee, put my earbuds in my ears and started typing about whatever it was on my mind.

I had never been a writer. I struggled writing term papers in college. At that time, two pages, double-spaced was difficult. But this time it was different. The words flowed like they never had before.

I quickly realized the difference between those term papers in college and what I was writing. The term papers required creating something from nothing. What I was doing was telling a story. I was merely taking the emotions that I had bottled up inside and put them on paper.

It was an emotional experience. There were tears flowing down my face as I typed. I was tucked away at a corner table in the back, so I didn't care.

Before I knew it, I was at 4 pages. It was the most vulnerable I have felt in a long time. At the same time, it was the most true and honest version of what I was going through. For once, I gave others an authentic look at who I was.

I re-read what I had written. It was pretty good. Even more, I felt better. I have never met with a psychologist before, but I can imagine the feeling was similar to that. There was a sense of relief that I was able to get the emotions out there.

I decided to publish it to a blog so others could follow along. It was much easier for me to type about what I was going through and publish it for everyone to read, instead of having to talk about it aloud dozens of times.

For the next couple months, I repeated this over and over, publishing new stories about our experiences every week. The response was amazing. I quickly developed a loyal following. Readers that would check back to follow along with our journey. Responses began to flow in. People shared words of encouragement, thoughts and prayers and some shared their own stories with me.

By sharing my story, I connected with them on a different level.

I decided to pull back on my business and focus my time on our personal issues for a while. I stopped searching for new clients. The one thing I continued, however, was writing my blog.

The strangest thing happened. Business began pouring in. Distant friends I hadn't talked to in a while reappeared. More than ever, my friends and family started referring their friends to me. Initially, I thought the uptick in business was because people felt bad for what we were going through. It was after a brief conversation with one of my new clients that I realized the true reason for the increase in business. He told me that the primary reason for him working with me was because he knew he could trust me to fight for his best interests.

It was eye-opening for me and led to a major change in the way I handled my business.

For years, I fought to keep my real estate business and personal life separate. Essentially, I was two different people. Some of my greatest clients and biggest supporters were people that knew me personally and professionally. As I reflected back on everything I had gone through and the response from those who read the stories I shared, I began to question why I kept the two separate.

My personal stories shaped who I was, both in business and in life. What was the point in censoring my personal life from my clients?

I began to share more personal stories. Some stories tied directly into my real estate business, while others didn't. Regardless, I shared them. It ended up being a turning point in my business. In the 12 months following Noah's birth, my business doubled over the previous 12 months.

I didn't spend any more time out looking for new clients. Instead, I focused on continuing the conversation with my current contacts. My daily interactions soon became subject matter for the content that I produced. The more and more they got to know the true me, the more they told their friends about me. Referrals started coming in faster than ever.

For the last two years, I have been an open book. No stories are off limits. I have never felt so free and, interestingly, business has never been better. I am confident there is a direct relationship between the two.

When I found out I was going to be a father for the first time, I knew my life was going to change. What I didn't realize at the time was that my unborn son would teach me one of life's greatest skills – the ability (and willingness) to tell my story.

- Kevin Evers

(Listen to Kevin's Interview on Podcast, between Ep 94 and 95)

<u>Recommended Resources:</u>

• **Protector Videos Series** (Access inside Member Site)

• **Case Study Interviews** (Access inside Member Site)

- **AMS Podcast** (www.AMSpodcast.com)

- **Value-Driven Approach** (www.TheValueDrivenApproach.com)

- **Forging Elite Storytellers** (www.StoryAthlete.com)

- **90-Day Immersion** (www.90DayImmersion.com)

- **Explore ImpactClub®** (www.ImpactClub.com)

Words from Carl Slade

My life fell apart…

Actually, self-destructed would be a more accurate description. Everything I'd worked hard to build, my family, my business, my finances… gone.

The 18 year marriage was over. Which, as I'm sure some of you will know, is a hard enough pill to swallow in itself, let alone seeing my children's lives turned upside down - through no fault of their own… Gut wrenching. Soul destroying. And my business? That was also in tatters. The team I'd trained, supported and handed clients to… were now my competition. Taking many of those clients with them.

What a shambles I had created. The errors of judgement, the shortsightedness, and lets face it, the completely brainless moments, still make me cringe.

Feelings of guilt and complete failure, weighed heavy. Depression, self-doubt, blame, being angry at the world - were now the demons to slay.

And the task of starting over, rebuilding, seemed daunting.

Did I even want to rebuild?

The answer to which became a resounding NO. No. I did not want to recreate the life I'd previously had.

Why?

Because it was not authentic to me. I was living a lie. Trying to be someone I was not... To please others? Perhaps. But happiness and fulfilment, were not dominant in my personal or business life. Which, by the way, I accept full and total responsibility for.

And that is precisely the silver lining.

I was forced to contemplate what I actually wanted to create, this time around. How I wanted my relationships to be? How I wanted my business to be? What I want to be known for? What's my higher purpose? Am I making the world a better place?

It's funny, when I attended our real estate group conference that year, seeking how to get my business back on track. The story was nothing new...

"Carl, just follow the proven path", they said.

Recruit, recruit and recruit some more. The bigger the pack out there hunting, the better. Keep them hungry on commission-only. Immerse them in the sales culture. Then train, train, train. Train them to prospect, to hustle - 100 cold calls a day. Train them to sell. To practice their scripts and dialogues. To always be closing. Success is judged on numbers of calls made, leads converted, listings won, commissions generated...

I knew in that moment that I could do it. I'd done it before. But I knew more of my soul would die. More of me will suffocate. Because I'd be doing something that - YES is proven to make money for some real estate businesses - but is not honest to me. I'd tasted that so-called 'success' ... it was hollow and fleeting.

That's when I challenged myself. I decided that I would build something different. That I would do things that will always be congruent to me. On what I stand for. On what I think is my true

nature. What I think will make the world a better place. I mean…
does it really need another typical real estate office? And once built, if
it disappeared the next day - would anyone really care? Would anyone
miss it?

Which is where my questioning of our industry began.

Why is it the way it is? How it works? What has it lead to? Its
poor reputation in the eyes of society. Why didn't I find personal
congruence in that path? Why prospecting, scripts, self-promotion,
manipulative closing techniques and high pressure tactics - to get a
commission - left me feeling somehow dirty?

It got me thinking about who I really am? What brings me peace,
contentment and fulfilment? When do I feel best, like I'm making a
difference, like I have a higher purpose?

I realized, that right from those early overweight childhood days, I
dislike bullies. At my core I'm a protector. Whether standing up for
smaller friends in the school yard or helping a client avoid costly
mistakes - many caused by our traditionally industry… that is my
purpose. Protecting, serving, genuinely adding value to others. That is
where my sense of self-worth is rooted.

A vision for a new world of real estate was born. Restating it, not
as a self-serving sales industry, but as a 'professional service'. Which
changes everything. How we work, our purpose, our culture, our core
values, the services we offer, the advice we give, our fees… the lot.

I could see an industry that protects and serves its clients. That
uses our specialist knowledge and skills to our clients advantage.
Truly helping them bank the most from their sale. An industry that's
not only respected, but more importantly, can be trusted. An industry
that adds genuine value to the community it serves, and as agents, we
feel proud to be a part of… My meaning was found and Restate Ltd
was launched in June 2015.

But something was still missing. A piece of the puzzle to find.
Something deeper and more significant. How was it that some
people, some companies, can massively improve the world, while

others, even with the best intentions, never get traction - they achieve very little?

This search lead me to Ryan, and the understanding of that missing piece…

The power of Story.

Understanding that the great influencers throughout history, have improved the world not with just their own deeds, but by encouraging & uplifting others to join the cause. They grew a following, a tribe, a movement of like-minded leaders working together for a common good.

They positively changed the world. Not through prospecting, trickery, gimmicks, sales scripts or bully tactics. But through authentically inspiring others.

This was a revelation for me. An exciting new skill to learn. But also a seemingly massive mountain to conquer. I'd never seen myself as a leader, a writer, a story teller. In fact 'English' was one of my worst subjects at school. And exposing my authentic self, my flaws, insecurities… showing others how I truly think… opening myself to criticism & judgement… well that was a scary thought.

Yet learning from Ryan, has helped me find my voice. The courage to share myself. The skills to grow. It's helped to totally transform my business…

With a small team we have proven our 'professional service' model to be not only sustainable, but more importantly significantly more efficient for both our clients and us as agents. Clients are banking, on average, around $4,800 more than with the traditional commission-only way, while we are more profitable. Most satisfyingly, the relationship with our clients is on a much higher level… It's a partnership. A 'Client' to 'Trusted Advisor' type relationship, rather than 'Prospect' vs 'Salesperson'.

Many of them are now becoming 'raving fans' - enthusiastically spreading the word, referring their friends and family. Their encouragement, support and written testimonials have been humbling. And as a team, we truly feel like we are making a real difference in our clients lives. We're fighting for something worthwhile.

Although the seed of a movement is planted, it's still early days... But the path is clear: becoming a better, more authentic 'story teller' is the way to inspire more of you to join the cause, slowly but surely spreading the message and helping to positively change the world of real estate.

So I invite you...

Because it's an obligation we have when we are able to do something good... When we share that good with the world, more good happens. And that's what we really want to do here. That is what Ryan has done for me. That is what he's teaching me to do for others. That is what I'd like to see you do also.

With that intention, I want to invite you to join in. To challenge yourself. To learn a new skill. To fully understand, what makes people really fall in love with you. What makes people want to join you in doing good. What makes people fans - of who you are as an individual, a company, a cause....

A purpose for good.

And...

'Story' - the ability to inspire others.

Those are the two keys to making a real difference. Those are the path to self-actualization. Those my friends, are the skills to teach our children - to ensure their fulfilment in the years ahead. And the best way to teach them, is to demonstrate to them, by learning, doing, and reaching our full potential ourselves.

Writing these very words would have been unthinkable for me just 18 months ago. Yet since then I've published countless articles, blog posts, even a book outlining our documented approach. They're not perfect by any means. But each day, each month, each new piece gets better.

I hope today, in these words, I've been able to connect with some of you on some level? Above all I hope I've been able to encourage you to believe in yourself. To find your own voice. To take the plunge and commit to a learning a life changing skill. A skill you can then share with others to inspire good.

Your past is done - Let it go.

Your future is a story yet to be written - by you.

Make it epic.

- Carl Slade

(Listen to Carl's Interview on Podcast, between Ep 98 and 99)

<u>Recommended Resources:</u>

• **Protector Videos Series** (Access inside Member Site)

• **Case Study Interviews** (Access inside Member Site)

• **AMS Podcast** (www.AMSpodcast.com)

• **Value-Driven Approach** (www.TheValueDrivenApproach.com)

• **Forging Elite Storytellers** (www.StoryAthlete.com)

• **90-Day Immersion** (www.90DayImmersion.com)

• **Explore ImpactClub®** (www.ImpactClub.com)

Words from Ryan France

Stories Are The Currency Of Life

I am not a man of many words… Spoken words that is. Put a pen in my hand or a keyboard at my finger tips and things can change rather quickly. But it hasn't always been that way.

For the better part of my career as a "Real Estate Agent," I looked at time spent writing, documenting and creating, as time spent away from my business. Rather than the fuel behind it.

For years, I wasted time trying to compensate for my perceived weaknesses rather than capitalize on my inherent strengths.

You see, by 'their definition,' I have no business being successful in real estate. I am not a great salesman. I am not a schmooze. I am not an extrovert, a phone shark or a politician. In fact, I never wanted to be a "Real Estate Agent," at all.

As a kid, my dreams were BIG. My future was bright. I was a ball player. A damn good one. A young man with a dream. A plan. A vision of one day following in the footsteps of his idols.

I never gave much thought to any particular path beyond my last day as a professional baseball player. And like many, I sorta just ended up in real estate.

For eight and a half years, I chased the allure of becoming a real estate titan. I modeled the schemes, the tactics, and the behavior of the mega-producers. I stuck a toe in the water with the who's who of real estate coaching.

And where did that get me?

I remember like it was yesterday. The first week in March, 2015. My two young children were playing on the floor in our upstairs game room. I was sitting on the coach with my wife. Noticeably troubled.

"What's going on?" she asked.

The only response I could muster was, "I don't think I can do this anymore. This just isn't me."

What I didn't tell her was that for a couple nights prior, I'd been scouring online job boards. In an odd way, that gave me some semblance of peace. Maybe there was a way out?

My soul was suffocating.

There had to be something else out there for me ... an opportunity that would to align my actual talents with a purpose. To make a bigger impact in my world. Surely I was not put on this earth to be just a "Real Estate Agent?"

Driving down to my office on the morning of my 35th birthday—later that month—the host of a podcast I was listening to posed the question, "Are you living the life today that you designed five years ago?" The only conclusion I could come was, "I don't know." A response that lacked conviction. I vowed on that morning, I would not allow myself to look back at 35 from 40 with the same indiscretion.

That same morning, I wrote: "I'm a firm believer that we are all put on this earth to make a certain meaningful contribution. We all have a calling, a purpose; yours different from mine. The lucky few find that calling from a young age. For others, it may take years or decades. Even some, it may never actually be realized.

I'm in relentless search of that calling. My calling. Sometimes I feel confident that I've found it and other times I can't help but feel that I'm not even scratching the surface. I certainly hope that I'm blessed enough to have a number of decades left to continue to find that voice. And yet, I feel strongly that at this very moment, my number is being called to step up, make a bigger impact and be a truer representation of who I am and what I believe.

As the world turns each year, there is no doubt that my sense of urgency increases. Questions I find myself asking: am I spending my time in direct (and appropriate) proportion to what matters most to me? Am I living up to my potential? Am I doing what inspires me? Am I living an authentic life? Am I inspiring others to do the same?

These are questions that deserve answers."

While I didn't recognize it at the time, what I lacked was not necessarily a purpose, as much as it was the skills needed (i.e. the toolkit) to start living that purpose into existence.

Not long after penning that post, I began to study the art of storytelling. Casually at first. Then more intensely, as I gained a greater and greater understanding of the power of a good story.

I've always been a pretty solid writer but I've come to learn that there is a distinct difference between simply writing something and actually delivering a message.

It's been said that stories are the currency of life. Of human contact and connection.

This point was driven home for me, clear as day, no more than two months after I made the commitment to start shedding my real estate skin and crafting a more empowering persona . . . through stories.

I was standing in the doorway of a house that I "put under contract," the day before. I was welcoming my client, Cyndi, to her new home. The catch was, she'd never seen the house and until then, we'd never met in person. Lots of phone calls and text messages but nothing face to face.

She and her husband were moving from California. I'd been working with her daughter, locally, to find the house. Never in a million years did I expect Cyndi to hop on a plane from California—on 18-hour notice—to be present for the home inspection.

As I shook her hand and we met for the first time, I told her how impressed and grateful I was that she'd made the effort. "Of course," she told me, "As soon as I read your biography (my personal narrative) and the articles on your website, I told my husband, this is a guy we are not going to let down." She went on and on thanking me, as if they had to earn MY trust instead of vice versa.

That was just one example, early on, of what has become quite common in my business over the past 2+ years.

Fletcher often says, as a real estate agent, you are hated before you arrive and distrusted before you've spoken a word. It's the penance of being associated with a negative reputation industry.

But as a storyteller things can change. Quickly and Drastically.

A new world opens up.

You begin to see a completely different path forward.

Just seven weeks after I joined the P/SS program, I wrote this message, to group members in Hipchat:

"I truly believe this group and what is being shared here is not only business-changing but can be life-altering in many respects. In the letter that I wrote to Ryan Fletcher before joining the program (that was read on the podcast), I mentioned that the past 6–12 months haven't been great for me and quite honestly, up until April of this year, if I was given the opportunity to go back and to start over, I WOULD NOT have done it again—chosen to be a Realtor. I was almost dead in the water mentally—just beaten down. Now, if given the opportunity to start over, my answer would be a resounding HELL YES! And I owe that 100% to shift in perspective, being able to be true to who I am and being surrounded by others (whom I've never met) that I already feel a kindred connection to. I look at guys like Eric Verdi and Ryan Sloper, who I'm sure were already successful in their own right but who have been on this path for 3 years and I am so excited about the vision of my business in 2–3 years. Because I know that I'll put in the work. Now, I just have an actual blueprint to work from. Thank you all!"

For the longest time I was afraid. Almost paralyzed by the thought of falling short of my potential. A fear of putting so much time, energy and effort into chasing their definition of 'success,' only to find out, at some critical point down the road, that I'd been firing at the wrong targets all along.

I don't think I can say it any better than Bob Goff already has, "I used to be afraid of failing at something that mattered to me. Now, I'm afraid of
succeeding at things that don't." According to 'them,' I'm probably still doing everything wrong. But frankly, I no longer care what they think because as a storyteller, I've begun to pen an entirely different definition of success.

One that echoes from an authentic voice.

This is me. I am at peace.

I have no doubt that I was put on this earth to be more than just a "Real Estate Agent."

Questions… Answered

- Ryan France

(Listen to France's Interview on Podcast, between Ep 57 & 58)

Recommended Resources:

• **Protector Videos Series** (Access inside Member Site)

• **Case Study Interviews** (Access inside Member Site)

- **AMS Podcast** (www.AMSpodcast.com)

- **Value-Driven Approach** (www.TheValueDrivenApproach.com)

- **Forging Elite Storytellers** (www.StoryAthlete.com)

- **90-Day Immersion** (www.90DayImmersion.com)

- **Explore ImpactClub®** (www.ImpactClub.com)

Words from Cheryl Gordon

Hey Ryan,

Just wanted to give you an update on how things are coming along…
I am currently in the process of collecting sponsorship donations
(currently over $5,000 collected) for Outdoor Movie Night for
Hunger™, as well as working with my ENG members on their
personal narratives as well as starting to see some great traction
regarding the teacher only donations! Everything seems to be falling
into place and I have you to thank for that!

I don't think I have said it enough but I am really excited and
proud to be a part of your Syndicate program. I am not sure if I
mentioned it but in the past, I have been a part of a few different
coaching programs…(Buffini and Maps Coaching). Neither of which
are anything like working with THE Ryan Fletcher.

I found in the past all of these "Real Estate" coaching programs

are all the same. Cold call, door knock, harass your friends and family, sleazy car salesmen like things that I have always hated.
I always thought there had to be a different way of doing things and I finally found that working with you. You have single handily helped me discover a new way of doing business and one that is more in line with what I want to do, and allows me to be doing business in a way that makes me proud. You have helped me create a newsletter people actually read... Helped me to better focus my business on its true purpose of being able to give back to my community... Helped me to create an awesome no-elevator-speech-required-networking-group, and have helped me take some of my good ideas, such as my Outdoor Movie Night for Hunger™ and make it better than I could have ever imagined!

It is amazing how you can take a good idea, Fletcher-ize it, and turn it into some extraordinary!

Other coaching programs I found to be very surface. They try to keep you on track and try to keep you accountable and motivated I guess but there was never any application. I always know that if I have an idea that I can bring it to you and the group and you will actually be hands on, give me ideas, examples, input, and ensure it reaches its full potential! But having said that it has been a lot of work on my part too. Obviously there has been some growing pains and a complete change in mindset. I am doing things I never thought where possible and, at times, things that made me extremely uncomfortable aka- my story!

It has been an amazing journey and I am starting to reap the rewards of all of the work I have put in so far... It's not easy to get this girl to change her ways... But you did it... and for that I am so grateful! I just wish I found your program sooner!

- Cheryl Gordon

Recommended Resources:

• **Protector Videos Series** (Access inside Member Site)

• **Case Study Interviews** (Access inside Member Site)

• **AMS Podcast** (www.AMSpodcast.com)

• **Value-Driven Approach** (www.TheValueDrivenApproach.com)

• **Forging Elite Storytellers** (www.StoryAthlete.com)

• **90-Day Immersion** (www.90DayImmersion.com)

• **Explore ImpactClub®** (www.ImpactClub.com)

Words from Tim "Spartan" Murphy

Crafting the Sword of a Spartan Warrior

Thank you for everything you do my friend. I wanted to give you a hug before I left.

This will have to do...

Fletcher, you have opened my eyes more than ever to the power of message. Now I feel myself molding my talents into a gifted messenger.   I'm not there yet... many years to go. But, I know each day I work on forging my sword... Finding only the perfect elements to melt and craft the strongest steel. Perfecting the art of removing all impurities which allow my sword to become unbreakable. Diligently forging a sword that is sharp, deadly and durable. All the while coating my sword with only the up most integrity and honor. These daily tasks, forge a curve in my sword unique to only me. Getting to this stage, in the forging of my sword, will take years. I know... Like you, one must believe in the power of words. I believe, people are attracted to those who believe what I believe.

From there I will polish my sword day in and day out... day, after day, after day. This process will never end. For those Spartan warriors who don't polish their sword will not be sharp. Without a sharp sword one cannot expect to lead the men of words. It will be after many, many years of polishing that one day I will add the final touches to my sword. It's these final touches which will create my LEGEND.

One of those final touches will be a mark for you my friend. Because without you entering into my life and opening my eyes.. I may have never taken the first step.

Love You!

Ooo-Rah! Spartan Warrior

- Tim Murphy

(Listen to Tim's Interview on Podcast, between Ep 95 and 96)

<u>Recommended Resources:</u>

• **Protector Videos Series** (Access inside Member Site)

• **Case Study Interviews** (Access inside Member Site)

• **AMS Podcast** (www.AMSpodcast.com)

• **Value-Driven Approach** (www.TheValueDrivenApproach.com)

• **Forging Elite Storytellers** (www.StoryAthlete.com)

• **90-Day Immersion** (www.90DayImmersion.com)

• **Explore ImpactClub®** (www.ImpactClub.com)

Words from Robert "Bob" Grand

Hey Bro,

I just wanted to say thanks again for believing in me.
ImpactClub® has again shown me what the right family is all about. I
was freaking out over my numbers for the club. It was a relief when
you guys showed up to walk me through the process.

I can honestly say this program is the toughest thing I've ever
done but you're a great guide. You aren't alone. I was scatter brained
that day just thinking about that event. It was my real first move away
from just people I know and an attempt to build something bigger. A
community of like-minded people. A community of givers. It was
awesome to have Lawrence come to the event also for support. This
is truly a real family of good people who care about each other's
success. I've said it before and I'll say it again, when I was in coaching
I was pissed every month I paid that 1k. In the P/SS Program I don't
even think about it. I learn so much from everything we do.

Speaking to other members in this group is the most valuable
education I can ever get. I instantly gained 30 news friends after the

event. These people are really excited to do great things in their community. I've always been civic minded and after the stress of launching wore off, I had an amazing sense of fulfillment.

Now that ImpactClub® is real in my community, the members have already said let's get this to 100+ people asap. It will happen! Thanks again brother. You and your team are awesome. Oh, and setting up those fucking lights was about the most fun I've had in long as time! I kept thinking shit these things are gonna fall soon.

Hahaha

P.S. it's the 4, 5, 6 Ryan. I have the most flexible commission structure IN the industry. It's amazing actually! Hahahaha

- Bob Grand

(Listen to Bob's Interview on Podcast, between Ep 102 and 103)

Recommended Resources:

• **Protector Videos Series** (Access inside Member Site)

• **Case Study Interviews** (Access inside Member Site)

• **AMS Podcast** (www.AMSpodcast.com)

• **Value-Driven Approach** (www.TheValueDrivenApproach.com)

• **Forging Elite Storytellers** (www.StoryAthlete.com)

• **90-Day Immersion** (www.90DayImmersion.com)

• **Explore ImpactClub®** (www.ImpactClub.com

RESOURCES

&

FREE GIFTS
OR NEARLY
FREE GIFTS

Resource & Free Gift

Gift #1 – Start <u>FREE</u> 7-Day Experience (www.StoryAthlete.com)

PRIVATE NETWORK: Association is powerful. If you hang out with "real estate agents," The Unethicals. The Incompetents. The Low-information agent. Then they, like your broker, will continually infect your thinking. You need a new Spartan Army to hang out with to develop new, bigger things. (This ties to the "Open Source" Movement to how Breakthroughs happen)

DAILY DISCUSSION: We are thinkers. We are strategic. We are methodical. To facilitate growth, we engage in daily discussion around central topics; Content, Distribution, Scale, and Impact. Within each of those quadrants, there are sub-quadrants (Not sales or prospecting) that lead to growth. (This ties to "Armies Must Be Inspired" & MTP: massive transformative purpose)

ACCESS TO FORMULAS: 1,000 True Fans. This is the only end-game. True Fans = Relationships. Relationships = Distribution Channels. Distribution Channels of a powerful message = Impact, and, as a by-product = Bottom-line (net) revenue growth. Once you understand the Formula to create True Fans. It's simply math. Every 100 new True Fans = An additional 6-figures. (This ties into "The Trend & Future of Marketing - Clean vs. "Unclean")

THE GAME IODs: Impact of the Day - Across Mind, Body, Business, Relationships. This is the critical component of Spiderweb Philosophy™, our proprietary content creation process, to capture hearts and minds. It starts with creating A-Stories, then tying that A to -BCDA - to dive business or cause. (This ties to the "Science" Borrowed From CrossFit® to create Sitcom-based content. Meaning, no more frustration or overwhelm. Just show up!!)

WEEKLY FEEDBACK SESSIONS (ADVANCED CONCEPTS): It should be obvious. We don't deal in the mundane or ordinary. You're here, and about to join this private network - of your own kind: dreamers, thinkers, visionaries who dare to execute against a Heroic Purpose - because you've been searching for something more than prospecting and sales. (Or the sickening "UN-clean" methods to grow a business, that destroy trust, and poison your soul!)

Start FREE 7-Day Experience:

www.StoryAthlete.com

Made in the USA
Columbia, SC
08 June 2019